What the critics say about
Sherman Yellen's *DECEMBER FOOLS*:

"The world is getting more brutish," trophy wife Gloria Temple tells her estranged daughter, Marcie. "And that makes art even more important." Perhaps playwright Sherman Yellen has expressed his own feelings in this dialogue, for this funny, touching and inspiring story of a mother and daughter coming to terms with their past is a perfect illustration of why art is important. *offoffonline.com*

Mr. Yellen, an old hand who has worked with theatrical greats like Richard Rodgers, peppers his script with amusing showbiz name-dropping, and the play has some delicious comic scenes, as when Gloria dishes out a New Yorker's dismantling of Santa Fe, N.M., where Marcie lives ("a place that's only suitable to someone in the witness protection program")... Mr. Yellen has provided that rarest of stage commodities: three strong roles for older women. In addition to Gloria, there are her hardheaded housekeeper and an old family friend named Mildred. *New York Times*

One of the funniest anti-smoking messages I've heard on or off stage is delivered half-way through Sherman Yellen's world-premiering *December Fools* by a one scene character who also happens to steal the show... "I was avant-garde. A little ahead of my time... I liked the good feelings of sex. So I fucked while you stayed pure and smoked your gold tipped Dunhills. And I was a scandal and you were the Lady Gloria. Only I still get around by myself while you lie there hooked up to hideous plastic tubes, struggling for every breath through that nasal thingamajig. Proves that fucking beats smoking any day of the week." *CurtainUp*

Also included in this collection of
New York plays by Emmy®-winning screenwriter
Sherman Yellen are two new works:
BUDAPEST and *GIN LANE*

Also From Moreclacke Publishing

Cousin Bella – The Whore of Minsk
by Sherman Yellen

The Flash of Midnight
by Robert Armin

DECEMBER FOOLS

and Other Plays

by

Sherman Yellen

December Fools ● *Budapest* ● *Gin Lane*

MORECLACKE PUBLISHING
New York City

Library of Congress Control Number: 2014905380

Moreclacke Publishing, New York, NY

ISBN-10: 0996016902

ISBN-13: 978-0996016902

Published in the United States of America

Moreclacke Publishing
325 West 45th Street, Suite 609
New York, NY 10036-3803
info@moreclacke.com

For Joan
who is the life of my love

Foreword

By Sheldon Harnick

Having collaborated with Sherman Yellen twice (on the musicals *The Rothschilds* and *Rex*), I thought I knew what to expect when I read this tripartite play collection: interesting, larger than life characters, intelligent, sophisticated dialogue spiced with wit and marked by an enviable command of language, expert stagecraft, and a sure-handed exploitation of the dramatic situations he had created. Nor was I disappointed; all of those elements are there aplenty.

What I didn't expect was the element of surprise, adroitly employed for dramatic effect. Both *The Rothschilds* and *Rex* are historical tales of real people in real situations. We had to assume that our audiences (at least those that were acquainted with the history involved) would expect these characters to travel on foreordained paths to predetermined destinations. Anything else would be falsifying history. Not so the three plays comprising *December Fools and Other Plays*. The characters in these plays, springing from Sherman's free-wheeling imagination, are free to act in unpredictable ways—and they do! In *December Fools* and *Gin Lane*, Sherman treats us to the gratification of unexpectedly upbeat endings, whereas, in *Budapest*, the major surprise (there are several) is a poignant, deliberately recognizable variation of one of the key scenes in *Camille*. And here I have to confess that Sherman had so thoroughly involved me in this drama, I had to assure myself that after the final curtain fell the telephone would ring, a desired conversation would ensue, and our heroine would be happy once again!

A word about the characters in these plays: they are complex, three-dimensional souls, part saint, part sinner. True, they tend to live in worlds most of us don't inhabit, with incomes we can only envy. This being so, one might think that their problems would be alien to us. Instead, Sherman's innate sense of compassion and his ability to people his plays with real human beings guarantee that their problems will register as intensified versions of our own. Consequently, we grieve with their sorrows and share their triumphs.

So here is my recommendation. Open a bottle of your favorite wine, settle down in your most comfortable chair and prepare to spend several enjoyable hours in the company of colorful, well-spoken people working their way through highly dramatic situations. You'll find, as I have, that time spent with Sherman Yellen is time well spent.

December Fools

DECEMBER FOOLS

A New Play
by Sherman Yellen

Gloria Temple, the beautiful widow of a renowned composer of musicals, has devoted her life to protecting her husband's name as a Broadway legend. In need of an heir apparent, she swallows her pride and summons her estranged daughter, Marcie, who fled to New Mexico years ago. While the rift between them deepens, Marcie stumbles upon a hidden cache of her mother's unmailed letters. Filled with dark secrets about her parents, her siblings – and herself – can Marcie resist payback?

The action of the play occurs in late December of 1983 in the foyer and library of Gloria Temple's Fifth Avenue apartment at the Sherry Netherland in New York City.

CHARACTERS

MARCIE TEMPLE SKLAR, daughter of Gloria Temple and of the late, great man; late forties to early fifties

MRS. HOGAN, Irish nurse-companion to Gloria Temple; late sixties

GLORIA TEMPLE, elegant, ailing widow of the late, great man; seventy

MR. PARKER-BENTON, the Smithsonian man; later as DR. ASHER, the psychiatrist; MAURICE, the hairdresser; and DR. LEWITT, the pulmonary specialist

VIVIAN, Englishwoman; mid fifties

MILDRED, strong, sophisticated woman; seventies

December Fools was first presented in New York City by the Abingdon Theatre Company at the June Havoc Theatre at the Abingdon Theatre Arts Complex. Previews began on January 27, 2006 and the play opened on February 1, closing on February 26 after 32 performances.

Production Staff: Donald Brenner (Director); Wally Harper (Original Music); William Cox (Arrangements); Susan Scherer (Costumes); James F. Wolk (Scenery); Matthew McCarthy (Lighting); Mary E. Leach (Production Stage Manager); Julie Griffith (Assistant Stage Manager).

Cast: Eric Michael Gillett (as Mr. Parker-Benton, Dr. Asher, Maurice, and Dr. Lewitt); Celia Howard (Mrs. Hogan); Mikel Sarah Lambert (Mildred); Carol Monferdini (Vivian); Arleigh Richards (Marcie Temple Sklar); Elizabeth Shepherd (Gloria Temple).

ACT I

(LIGHTS UP on MARCIE SKLAR, an attractive, sturdy looking, middle-aged woman, standing in the penthouse foyer, being greeted by MRS. HOGAN, her mother's Irish nurse companion. She hands the woman her umbrella and a wet raincoat, takes off a plastic rain scarf and shakes out her hair. The hallway has a Lalique vase filled with white roses. Here, as in the library we soon enter, we find the elegant taste of an apartment furnished in the 1930s.)

MRS. HOGAN

Mrs. Sklar, thank God you're here. Wet, but wanted. And just in time.

MARCIE

Mother?

MRS. HOGAN

No. It's the Smithsonian man. I told him he could only have her for a half hour. He agreed, and now he's taken her for nearly two.

MARCIE

Just tell him to go, Catherine.

MRS. HOGAN

You try it. Twice I've asked him to leave. He won't hear a simple "please go." Those theatre scholars are such lying devils. And the government ones are the worst. If that wasn't bad enough, Dr. Lewitt's waitin' for us at the hospital. She's due for her examination in twenty minutes.

MARCIE

I thought he came to the apartment for that.

MRS. HOGAN

Ya can't bring all that diagnostic equipment here. She's obliged to go to hospital like everyone else.

MARCIE

She can't like that.

MRS. HOGAN

She's too much the lady to complain.

MARCIE

Yes. Too much the lady.

MRS. HOGAN

You know I say a perpetual prayer for her recovery.

MARCIE

I guess I should put a stop to it.

MRS. HOGAN

(Confused)

The prayer?

MARCIE

(Dryly)

The interview, Catherine.

(MARCIE crosses into the library and enters the room. Her mother, GLORIA TEMPLE, a beautiful woman of seventy sits in front of a microphone and tape recorder set up on a library table, a plastic tube extends from her nostrils to an oxygen tank at the other end of the room. A thin, scholarly looking man, MR. PARKER-BENTON, sits perched on a bench nearby.)

GLORIA

For most people, '37 was a dreadful year. Protests and unemployment, violence in the steel mills, Hitler and his chamber of horrors –

MARCIE

Mother!

GLORIA

(To MARCIE)

Darling, you're here. Good. Make yourself comfortable. We've just reached Hitler, and I promised the Grand Inquisitor I would take him through 1937 this afternoon.

(To PARKER-BENTON)

Everything was so serious. Even Broadway. Why *Pins and Needles* was a big hit! Imagine? A musical comedy produced by garment workers. But that was the world then –

(She begins a fragment of a song from Pins and Needles *and he joins in.)*

GLORIA (Continued)

"Sing me a song of social significance, all other songs are taboo!" It was a grim time.

(She laughs ruefully.)

PARKER-BENTON

But not for Temple and Blake?

GLORIA

No. That was the year they were working on *The Girl Said Yes*, a marvelous bit of fluff. They tried to get Ginger to come back to Broadway to star in it, but she was already on a winning streak with the Astaire films, *so that girl said no.*

PARKER-BENTON

But Merman said yes?

GLORIA

Unfortunately. Two days into rehearsal, the Merm turned.

PARKER-BENTON
(Laughing)
Is that how Mr. Temple put it?

GLORIA

I'd never let you quote me on what Alex actually said!
(They laugh conspiratorially.)
He was furious.

PARKER-BENTON

What really happened between them?

GLORIA

Ethel wanted that lovely ballad Alex had written for the ingénue, despite the fact that it made no sense for her to sing it. So Alex said, "Screw her!" And she "ankled tunesical," as *Variety* put it. "Let Cole or Dick or Irving deal with her," Alex told Jack; but still, he loved her talent. He so admired the way she planted her feet on the stage and fired away with a song.

PARKER-BENTON

Wasn't there talk of Ann Sothern coming in to replace her?

GLORIA

Yes, Ann could sing, ya know. But they finally decided to give the lead to an unknown, the pretty little understudy. I can't recall her name but if you give me a moment –

PARKER-BENTON

Benita Heywood?

GLORIA

Yes, yes, little Benita Heywood. Pretty round face. Big button eyes. And her voice, quite true and pleasing.

PARKER-BENTON

Whatever happened to her?

GLORIA

Died a few years ago in Hollywood. Car crash? Or was it pills? Read it somewhere – *The Times*, I think? Yes, *The Times*. I suppose she's in ingénue heaven, batting those button eyes at St. Peter. Yes, it was a great hit.

PARKER-BENTON

Their fourth in a row.

GLORIA

It was a great year for the boys. And a marvelous one for me too. My daughter, Marcella was born that year. Marcie's just come to visit me from New Mexico.

(She gestures towards MARCIE.)

Marcie Sklar, Mr. Parker-Benton. Mr. Parker-Benton is preparing material for an exhibition at the Smithsonian devoted to Daddy's work.

PARKER-BENTON

Mrs. Sklar. A pleasure.

MARCIE

A short one, I'm afraid. Time's up. Mother, you look tired.

PARKER-BENTON

Next Monday, Mrs. Temple?

GLORIA

(All stops out on her charm)

I wouldn't think of leaving you forever mired in the Depression. But the war years were so exciting; they're likely to do me in.

PARKER-BENTON

Mrs. Temple. Mrs. Sklar.

(He exits carrying his tape recorder and satchel.)

MARCIE

Mother, you really can't keep giving these interviews. They'll kill you.

GLORIA

Nonsense. Nobody dies from wonderful memories. Darling, that man is so greedy. Whenever I show him some of Daddy's handwritten scores, the private letters, the Hirschfield caricatures, I can spot the shoplifter's glint in his eye.

MARCIE

I'm sure you protect them with your life.

(She shakes out her unruly hair.)

GLORIA

How was your trip? Silly question, all plane trips are awful. Even when they land safely, they wreck the skin and the hair. You've always had such pretty hair. Still do. But it would look so much better if you didn't color it. Yourself. Makes it coarse and fools no one, you know?

MARCIE

(Annoyed)

You should write a book of beauty advice, Mother. Why waste it on me?

GLORIA

I did. *Gloria Temple's Guide to Good Grooming.*

MARCIE

Yes. Yes. I forgot. Mrs. Hogan says that you have an appointment at the hospital. Would you like me to go to the doctor with you?

GLORIA

No, you must be tired. And Mrs. Hogan is quite capable of riding shotgun beside me in the ambulette.

MARCIE

Shall I call Dr. Lewitt and tell him you'll be late?

GLORIA

No. Let him wait for the pleasure of pushing my poor chest against the cold x-ray plate.

MARCIE

I'd have thought you'd want to get it over with and –

GLORIA

There we differ. Nothing I like so much as avoiding the unpleasant. You, on the other hand, always welcomed your misery with open arms.

MARCIE

(Opening her arms in greeting)

Hello, Mother. So happy to see you.

GLORIA

That's unkind.

MARCIE

Why'd you call me home?

GLORIA

(Ignoring the dig, trying to get beyond it)

I wanted to see *you.* It's been months. How's the painting going? I loved the exhibition postcard. I look at it when I need something bright to cheer me up. Now, how much longer will you be living in that dreary place?

> *(GLORIA takes a drag on the oxygen as if it was a cigarette, and reconnects the plastic nose grip.)*

MARCIE

Santa Fe?

GLORIA

Yes. I wonder if your Santa Fe was a distant connection of the famous Fay family. There was Joey Fay, Frank Fay, Francis Fay, Fay Wray, and of course the adorable Alice, the Faye of all Fays. But who the hell was Santa Fe?

MARCIE

Okay, it's not for you. But I love New Mexico.

GLORIA

How can you? You're not second-rate.

MARCIE

I don't rate people. Or places.

GLORIA

Fine. Don't. They have a way of doing that by themselves. But places do require some discrimination.

MARCIE

When were you there? Thirty years ago? For two days? You don't know enough about it to have an informed opinion.

GLORIA

What is there to know? It's a place for a day trip, darling. Not for a lifetime.

MARCIE

If you saw the sky from my ranch after a storm you might change your mind.

GLORIA

Never. I couldn't stand all that exuberant scenery. That vast blue sky and the thin air made me dizzy and stirred up my migraines. Do you sleep with Indians there?

MARCIE

(Dryly)

Of course. But only with Chieftains from your better tribes.

GLORIA

Joke, but you know it's the kind of place that attracts drifters with no roots of their own.

MARCIE

It also draws people who want clean, cool air, wonderful light, and a decent, simple life. And a few fools like me who want to be artists.

GLORIA

You're a born and bred New York Jewish woman. It's a pity you feel the need to escape that.

MARCIE

I have no intention of denying my heritage – or returning to New York.

GLORIA

What if I asked you to stay awhile with me now?

MARCIE

How long is your "awhile?"

GLORIA

At least through Christmas. New York is so wonderful at Christmas.

MARCIE

Mother, you know I hate it here.

GLORIA

(Sarcastically)

So you prefer Santa Fe, a place that's only suited for someone in the witness protection program?

MARCIE

New York has changed more than you know. On my way over in the taxi we were stuck in traffic in front of a Gap, that's a clothing chain –

GLORIA

I know what it is darling. Mrs. Hogan is always buying tee shirts there for her blessed grandchildren.

MARCIE

I saw this crazy derelict woman, dressed all in rags, standing in the freezing rain, applying mascara to her puffy eyes in the reflection of the store window. It was so cold outside I was scared she'd freeze to death.

GLORIA

Yes? So what did you do?

MARCIE

I felt sick. And sad.

GLORIA

Go back a bit. You saw this poor deranged woman grooming herself in a shop window? Did you stop the taxi and offer her money so she could find shelter for the night?

MARCIE

No.

GLORIA

But you had feelings. Well, damn all feelings. At the end of the day, it's what *we do*, not what *we feel* that matters. Why, in the Depression, when I was moved by the pitiful lot of the Negro children in this city, I didn't drive on in my limousine and feel pity. I set up a nursery school with free meals in Harlem. It took me away from my work and my family but it was worth it.

MARCIE

Oh, the sacrifices you made to make the world a little brighter.

GLORIA

You can mock me all you wish but I did something that had to be done!

MARCIE

The man from the Smithsonian's gone. I know just how good you are.

GLORIA

No, my dear. I'm not that good. I'm just not that bad. Don't imagine I don't know why you hate New York. You used to adore it.

MARCIE

Don't!

GLORIA

Please. It's been twenty years.

MARCIE

As they warned on the old maps, *"Terra Incognita.* Traveler beware."

GLORIA

Time you put it all behind you. Aren't they punished enough?

MARCIE

Really? How?

GLORIA

They are condemned to live in Cal-ee-phonya. I hate to think of anyone I ever loved living there.

MARCIE

You think of them often, don't you?

GLORIA

It's what one does living alone. I think of everyone I've lost. My father, my husband, my son. And Vivian. Yes, Vivian.

MARCIE

Mother, what do you want? You left a message on my machine, demanding that I drop everything and fly out to you at once. Why am I here?

GLORIA

To take over from me as head of the Alexander Temple Foundation.

MARCIE
(*Shaking her head vigorously*)

No. No. No.

GLORIA

There's only you.

MARCIE

What about Stanley?

GLORIA

Stanley? He is a wonderful lawyer, but with his woeful taste in neckties and wives, I hardly think he's the man to judge a theatre grant application. These are dreadful times. With Ronnie in the White House, indifference and cruelty pass for charm and morality. And that wife, that Nancy of his, why her adoring expression as she looks at him, it's... it's sickening.

MARCIE

It reminds me of how you used to look up at Daddy.

GLORIA

But Daddy *was* adorable. Darling, are you so cut off from the world in your Santa Fe that you don't know that dreadful things are happening all over? Did you know that *Time Magazine* has named the computer – yes the computer – Man of the Year? People don't matter these days and neither does art. Someone named Toto – trust me on this – Toto – won the Grammy Award. And if that wasn't bad enough, *Cats* has won the Tony.

(Disgusted)

Cats! Why did they put it in a theatre when all it needed was a litter box?

MARCIE

Did you see it?

GLORIA

How can I? I can't go to theatre connected to all my breathing apparatus.

MARCIE

If you haven't seen it, how can you be so sure you wouldn't like it?

GLORIA

I've listened to the recording – on one of those little compact disks. Make a note. We must see to it that all of Daddy's shows are transferred on to them as soon as possible. You can squeeze more of his songs into one little disk – it's amazing. Yes, we must –

MARCIE

Mother, I am not making notes. I am not working at the Foundation. I *will not* be working for the Foundation. Not now. Not ever. There's no reason for me to do so – other than your wanting me to –

GLORIA

But there is. You have excellent taste. You love fine art and good music. Working for the Temple Foundation you'd be able to encourage and support new talent. We need to help the new artists. All the old brilliant ones are dying like flies this year. Last month poor Tennessee dropped, before him that darling Joan Miro, yesterday Bucky Fuller –

MARCIE

I've lost you somewhere between compact disks and the obituary page.

GLORIA

What I'm trying to say is that the world is getting nastier and more brutish and that makes art more important.

MARCIE

Everyone's art, but mine?

GLORIA

This isn't about you. It's about Daddy and his work.

MARCIE

It always is, isn't it?

GLORIA

You want it to live on, to be valued for what it was, *what it is!* You can still paint your pretty pictures while you run the Foundation. Marcie, I am desperate.

MARCIE

Would you ask me to do this if you respected my work?

GLORIA

I happen to think you're a splendid painter. You may not be up there with the masters, but nobody is, including most of the masters. Why, when I illustrated my children's books, I knew I was no master, but it was enough for me just to be good.

MARCIE

Mother, you've asked before. And I said no. How many times must I –

GLORIA

Marcie, I'm truly desperate!

MARCIE

And I'm truly sorry. But I've worked hard to gain a measure of peace. Too hard to have you destroy it now by making me come back to New York.

GLORIA

Privilege has its responsibilities.

MARCIE

I'm happy to spend the holidays with you, but I'll be returning to Santa Fe after the New Year. Trust me on that.

GLORIA
(Sadly)

Yes, I do.
(MRS. HOGAN enters holding GLORIA's coat out for her.)

MRS. HOGAN

Mrs. Temple, the driver is waiting. God knows what he's charging you for that. You must go now.

GLORIA

As soon as I freshen up. I'll be with you in a minute.

MRS. HOGAN

Shall I come with you?

GLORIA

I am still capable of passing water unassisted.

(GLORIA exits alone.)

MARCIE

Nothing ever changes here, does it?

MRS. HOGAN

No. Thank goodness. Is there anything you'll be needin' while we're gone?

MARCIE

Yes, Catherine. I came here in such a hurry I left with checks to write, letters to answer, and a birthday note to get out to a friend. Do you know where mother keeps her stationery and stamps?

MRS. HOGAN

Well, there's some inside the desk. But it's locked.

MARCIE

The key should be on the key rack inside the hall closet.

MRS. HOGAN

Yes. That pretty silver one with a silk tassel. Madam puts such swank into everything.

MARCIE

(Sarcastically)

Such swank.

MRS. HOGAN

And she's so wonderfully organized. I'll go find it for you.

(MARCIE walks around the library; she studies a framed Hirschfield drawing of her father, a silver framed photograph of her parents in their early forties, her mother gazing lovingly on her father. She glances around the shelves of LP recordings and puts one on the phonograph. A lilting melody is heard. It is played throughout the scene, only ending with the reading of the letter. MRS. HOGAN returns, brandishing the key with its tassel.)

MRS. HOGAN

Here it is.

MARCIE

Thank you.

MRS. HOGAN

I'll be going down to the letterbox on the corner with Madam's mail late this afternoon. I can mail yours as well when you're ready.

(GLORIA returns. She lets herself be bundled into the coat. MRS. HOGAN puts her scarf around her throat; GLORIA rearranges it to suit herself.)

GLORIA

Try to rest, darling. And think over what we discussed.

MARCIE

Mother, there's really nothing to think over. I can't return here.

GLORIA

No, I suppose you can't, if you can't. Come, Mrs. Hogan, the dungeons of Columbia Presbyterian await us.

(We watch MARCIE as she places the key in the drawer and opens it. She takes out a stack of writing paper, sees a small packet of letters on blue note paper tied with a ribbon. She unties the ribbon, opens a letter, unable to contain her curiosity. In the transitions we hear the piano playing show tunes, music of Alex Temple, melodic, romantic, optimistic; songs of another time, another place; songs heard from a distance, as if through a closed door.

LIGHTS down on MARCIE, up on GLORIA, now a younger, more vigorous version of herself. As MARCIE reads a letter, DR. ASHER, a psychiatrist, seated at a desk, deep in mimed conversation with a younger GLORIA. MARCIE reads the letter aloud and soon GLORIA takes over the reading of the letter. Throughout the reading of these letters, there is a blending of the voices; this is a duet, with the occasional sound of another instrument, the other voice adding another note. Sometimes the two women read separately, other times in unison, sometimes overlapping, varying the texture of the letters. The music of Alex Temple is interwoven throughout. MARCIE begins to sound more like her mother as she reads and her Mother regains the youth and vitality of the time when many of the letters were written.)

MARCIE

(Reading aloud)

Dear Dr. Asher. This week I came to your office on the advice of my husband's lyricist, Jack Blake, seeking help for my terrible migraine headaches. I have never been to a psychiatrist's office before, and I would never have gone, if not for my headaches which seem to resist all analgesics.

MARCIE and GLORIA

Jack assured me that you were a very wise man...

GLORIA
(Taking over)

...and a great help to him, and I am desperate with a pain that needs more than aspirin. He said you don't dawdle about trying to open locked rooms over months and years, but get to the point quickly.

MARCIE and GLORIA

And my headaches demand immediate attention.

DR. ASHER

Would you lie down on the couch, Mrs. Temple?

GLORIA

No, the chair is fine, Doctor. I'm here for a consultation, not a course of psychoanalysis.

DR. ASHER

Why not let me judge what is best for you?

MARCIE

After a few minutes of conversation, you did just as Jack promised you would. You gave me your diagnosis of the cause of my headaches.

DR. ASHER

My dear Mrs. Temple, it is your excessive control over your anger that's turned inward and caused these so-called migraines. You can never hope to be released from the terrible pain you suffer until you learn to express your anger, your rage.

GLORIA

How? Women of my generation were taught to turn away from those who had injured them, to cut them out of their lives, not to engage in the open expression of anger.

DR. ASHER

Look, if you can't express your rage, I can't help you.

GLORIA

You want me to shriek like a fishwife and throw plates at people?

DR. ASHER

Is that how you avoid things? By bringing them to ridiculous extremes? Here's something that even you can do. Write out your angry feelings in letters addressed to those who hurt you.

GLORIA

Impossible. Imagine opening up the morning mail and reading some screed from Gloria Temple. "That Gloria must have gone mad!" Well I haven't, so I won't.

DR. ASHER

Did I say you have to mail 'em? The idea is to ventilate the anger, open your sealed windows, let in the air. Keep the letters safely hidden away as a record of your deepest emotions, a place to store your fury, outside that poor throbbing head of yours.

GLORIA

Well, I could do that. I could, couldn't I?

DR. ASHER

You could. But the migraines are just a symptom. Tell me more about your family.

MARCIE
(Back in letter style)

So I told you all about my family and my pain. Would it surprise you that the anger I feel today is directed towards you? I came to your office seeking comfort for my pain and what did I receive? Blame. Judgment! Even scorn! Whereas my son's success in school is his own doing, my daughter Marcie's misconduct, her cheating, her tantrums, are all the result of my not loving her properly.

DR. ASHER

Of course she feels unwanted by you! Let me see her picture.

(GLORIA fumbles in her pocketbook and produces picture.)

GLORIA

Cute, isn't she?

DR. ASHER

I've seen cuter.

GLORIA

What?

DR. ASHER

She's not a pretty child, and you're a beautiful woman. Let me see the little British refugee? Now that's a beauty. Life gives you the klutzy one, so you find yourself a dainty little British war orphan to take into your home, a lovely Princess doll to play with. Why shouldn't Little Miss Klutz act up? So what does the husband think of this?

GLORIA

Alex lets me run the family as I think best.

DR. ASHER

Face the hard truth, Mrs. Temple. You're a lucky woman. You look like a million bucks; better yet, you have a million bucks. And your husband's a magician, an alchemist who sits at a piano and turns tunes into money. He goes from hit show to hit show and takes you along for the ride. We call that a great life. Say it, "I have a great life!"

GLORIA
(Pointedly misunderstanding)

You have a great life.

DR. ASHER

You're one tough cookie, aren't you? Why don't you bask in the glory that your husband brings to you? Why do you insist upon making yourself sick with your busy-work as a children's book illustrator? Your pictures? They're cute but –

GLORIA

You've seen cuter?

DR. ASHER

And your charities? Busy, busy, busy, busy, busy. You flit from one good deed to another. Schweitzer has nothing on you but the moustache and the bushy white hair. So you love the world? Big deal. It takes more character to love your own.

GLORIA

Excuse me, Doctor Asher, I have to use the bathroom.

ASHER

How old are you?

GLORIA
(Surprised)

Thirty-seven.

ASHER

You've peed enough.

GLORIA

What?

ASHER

Sit still, Mrs. Temple! I want your attention, not a urine specimen.

MARCIE
(Reading as Gloria)

So I listened as Sigmund Freud met Smith and Dale. As you spoke, I saw a small, ugly, toad, envious of beauty, talent, and wealth; a false healer who does not comfort suffering, but seeks control over the lives of his famous patients with insults that pass for insights. You are an utter failure and a fucking fraud.

GLORIA
(In reading mode)

Never, never, never will you gain control over my life. But there must be something to your advice. After all, I do feel better for having written this letter and I will not mail it on the advice of my doctor. My secretary, Miss Himmelman will call tomorrow and cancel our future appointments. She will say that, "Unfortunately, Mrs. Temple has a terrible headache." I will never see you again. I can suffer my migraines far easier than I can suffer you. I'd rather light a candle to Theresa, the patron saint of headaches, or consult the entrails of a dead chicken, than look to you for advice. Very truly yours, Gloria Klineman Temple.

MARCIE
(Reading another letter)

Dear Mildred, you think I am blind? That I have no idea you slept with Alex when I was away at the Essex farm with the children? Returning to the city yesterday I found your earring in my bed.

GLORIA

I knew at once it was yours.

MARCIE

Like you, the earrings were expensive and ridiculous. Irrefutable evidence of what you had done with Alex. I had forgotten your reputation as the woman who introduced and pioneered fellatio on the Upper East Side. West of Lexington and Sixty-Fifth Street...

GLORIA

...up to Fifth and Ninety-Sixth.

MARCIE

Always the first to style your hair in the latest fashion…

GLORIA

…and the last to know how awful you look in it.

MARCIE

Try as you will, you're still stuck with being Millie Wurtz, a dirty joke with an enormous income…

GLORIA

…and a bottom to match.

MARCIE

Don't delude yourself. It was hardly a love affair, just one more unsavory interlude in your sordid life.

GLORIA

How I pity you.

MARCIE

You made a bad bargain.

GLORIA

You won't get Alex and you've lost both a costly earring and a priceless friend. Gloria.

MARCIE

Dear Maurice, when I went to your salon yesterday prior to having my portrait photograph taken with my husband for the *Life Magazine* cover, I asked you to…

GLORIA

…just trim and set my hair but please, please do nothing that makes me look unnatural.

MAURICE

Why would I do that, Mrs. Temple? I know your hair. But nothing is more aging than yesterday's hairdo. Trust me. You'll love it.

GLORIA

Remember, we're being photographed in profile. Alex has always admired the line of my forehead. So it should –

MAURICE

It will!

MARCIE

When I was finally allowed to look at myself in the mirror, I was horrified.

GLORIA

What's that on my head?

MAURICE

A feather cut.

GLORIA

A what-a-cut?

MAURICE

It's the new do. For the new you. CZ and the Duchess both had me do it, and they look years younger. Doesn't she look years younger, Leonard? Yes, it's perfect for your face. Hides your big forehead and conceals those furrows of yours, best of all it cuts the length of your long face and softens your chin.

GLORIA

My chin needs softening?

MAURICE

It's like an instant lift, only without the scalpel and the pain, just Maurice's magic scissors. Give it a day. You'll love it.

MARCIE
(Reading letter)

And so I left your shop…

GLORIA

…head feathered…

MARCIE

…chin softened…

GLORIA

…forehead covered…

GLORIA and MARCIE

…utterly miserable.

MARCIE

Maurice, I have given it a day. A very long day. And I miss my long forehead. Feathers are for poultry…

GLORIA

…and I am neither a chicken…

MARCIE

…nor a goose.

GLORIA

But there's no denying…

MARCIE and GLORIA

...you are a butcher.

MARCIE

I thought you were an artist, a craftsman, and a collaborator in helping me to be myself.

GLORIA

Instead you are a vandal armed with scissors.

MARCIE

Although I will continue to come to your salon; after all you do keep appointments on time...

GLORIA

...never eat garlic...

MARCIE

...don't gossip...

GLORIA

...and keep a spotless salon...

MARCIE

...I shall always remember how you disfigured me at an important time in my life.

(*MARCIE starts to flip through the letters, reading the next one aloud.*)
My dear Mrs. Hogan, it is one thing to pray and light candles for me to your god of perpetual pain, quite another to share the details of my illness with the elevator operator and anyone who performs the smallest service for me. I was well within earshot of your latest tittle-tattle about my health. Now spread through the building by the elevator man.

MRS. HOGAN

She hasn't long, ya know? Don't mention it to anyone, dear, but the lungs are quite worn out, they are. It's that airway obstruction! A permanent enlargement of her "alveolar air spaces." Those alveolar walls of hers, poor dear – totally destroyed. We won't talk of that shadow on her lung. The heart can take only so much and the rest of her is breakin' down quicker than it can be propped up by me and Doctor Lewitt – but bless her, she's a brave little soldier she is.

MARCIE

Mrs. Hogan, I asked only that you respect my privacy; since dying for me is a very private matter. And you have violated it with your wagging Hogan tongue. You are a fortunate woman, so I understand why you count your blessings like a rosary.

GLORIA

You have children and grand-children who honor you for the money you send home to them…

MARCIE

…children who will love you as long as you ante up the birthday bounty…

GLORIA

…the Gap clothes…

MARCIE

…and the Toyota motorcars.

MARCIE and GLORIA

They are greedy…

GLORIA

…cross-eyed…

MARCIE

…fat cheeked louts…

GLORIA

…shrewd bumpkins who have turned you, their mother and grandmother, into their cash cow.

MARCIE

How often they must toast your health with a jar of whisky. Today I will speak to you in the softest, kindest manner…

GLORIA

…God knows anything else will bring down Jesus, Mary, and all kinds of saints on my head…

MARCIE

…and tell you that I would consider it a kindness if you did not discuss my failing health with others. I need you too much to send you away for exercising the Hogan mouth. I shall tell you to conceal the nature and severity of my illness because it only makes me sad to know that I will soon lose the company of so many good friends…

GLORIA

…and servants.

MARCIE

Yours…

MARCIE and GLORIA

…Gloria Temple.

GLORIA

My dear Alex, I am writing this from the farm in Essex. Strange, I've always wanted to be in New York when troubles came. But this time it is too much for me. Marcie was so distraught I told her to stay on in the city for a while, that we could do nothing for each other. Vivian, who is more composed, asked to accompany me to the farm, so she is here now, administering the sedatives and reading to me. I don't think I've ever had so many cups of tea in my life. Tea and Nembutal. This will be the first of your openings I will not attend. I know you would have liked me to be there, beside you, to put a brave face on our tragedy, but I can't do it. I've run out of brave faces.

MARCIE

Somehow, the project seemed cursed from its inception. First there was the casting of Sir Philip Cowles as Disraeli. A great classical actor, with a dry tuneless singing voice, who could do little justice to what is at best a mediocre score. Whatever were you thinking? So imperious was he, more regal than your young Victoria, who Sir Philip had seduced early in the rehearsals. A commonplace event, commonplace as her talent, small and cheerful but hardly enough to command the stage. Our Terry, eighteen, working as your personal assistant, working on a Broadway show for the first time and loving every moment of it.

GLORIA

He has… he had so many talents. Had he lived, I think he might even have surpassed you. But we will never know that now. Never. I read the police report and I don't believe a word of it. How Terry was celebrating at that Halloween party being given by the cast, and how he had become dizzy, opened a window for some air and accidentally fell to his death. Death by dizziness. Runs in my family. My father was dizzy when he tumbled in front of a moving subway train, after losing his fortune in the First War. You alone, among the men in my life, had learned how to survive. You alone are never dizzy. Oh, the advantages of a childhood in the slums where one learns to sharpen ones elbows and one's wits to live. A pity you did not teach that to Terry. Terry and Daddy. Both suicides. As one gets older we relive the old sorrows in the current grief. So this one is unbearable – it fuses my past and my future. Marcie was very much your daughter... but Terry... was... my son.

MARCIE

I have pieced together what happened from the gossip that has come to me from the grieving cast, and from Sir Philip himself. He said that most of the chorus boys had raided the costume department for gowns worn by the ladies-in-waiting to Victoria. Someone must have dared poor Terry to join in the dress-up. Surely we both knew what our son was. We deluded ourselves because he had inherited your skills at sports – and my good looks – which drew the girls to him, but he was marked by his leanings from the earliest age. We denied what we suspected, but we always knew. He was too compliant, and that is dangerous in a man. And I now know that you killed Terry.

GLORIA

When you walked into the cast party seeking your young Victoria, offering her a new song as a way to get her into your bed, you saw your eighteen year old son, made up, bewigged and bedizened, dressed as a girl of Victoria's court, dancing with another boy dressed as a court lady, dancing to a rock and roll recording. What disgusted you more, the sight of Terry in drag or the sound of that music? Poor Terry, did he come towards you to greet you, forgetting in his drink and hilarity the way you would react?

MARCIE

Was he testing you, seeing if your love for him could absorb all this and still survive?

GLORIA

Did you walk towards him and whisper in his ear as Sir Philip maliciously reported. "Wipe off that makeup. Get yourself cleaned up you little prancing fairy." Did you add, "I am so goddamned ashamed of you. I wish you were never born"?

MARCIE

At that point, Sir Philip reports, the boy opened the window, and fell to his death twelve floors below. Now, he might have been dizzy. It was quite warm in there. He had been drinking. He could have been dizzy. Believe that, if you wish. So, Alex, when Terry killed himself, was he just trying to please you one last time? Now we shall be partners in another lie – far greater than all your infidelities – Terry's death.

GLORIA

Oh, if I could only stop missing him, or better yet, stop loving you. I shall study how to love you less in the years to come, but I will fail the course. Gloria.

> (MARCIE *is deeply moved by the letter. She goes towards the desk with it when her eye hits on another letter which she picks up.*)

MARCIE

Dear Dr. Lewitt. Last week, when I came to the hospital for your torturous tests and murderous treatments, you were quick to give me the report.

DR. LEWITT

If you look at that area of the left lung, the dark spot on the lower right, you'll see what I've been talking about.

GLORIA

Can nothing be done?

DR. LEWITT

Nothing. You could never survive a surgery. And if you did, the chances are –

GLORIA

How long do I have?

DR. LEWITT

A month. Perhaps two. It could be a bit more, a bit less.

GLORIA

(Protesting)

But I still have so many good days. How can I be dying?

DR. LEWITT

You'll have your ups and your downs, and finally – just downs. That's how we die.

GLORIA

(Ruminating on the word)

Dying! How... wasteful. What happens to all the French and the Italian we've learned. All the love we've felt. All the songs we know. I suppose we die like Pharaohs, and take our treasures with us to the grave. Will you call my daughter and tell her?

DR. LEWITT

Don't you think that should come from you?

GLORIA

I've been trying to get her to come back to New York for years. I don't think she'll believe me if this comes from me. I need her to be with me now, Doctor. I don't want to die... but if I must, I don't want to die without my daughter near me.

DR. LEWITT

You told me that you two didn't get along. Why suffer the strain of her company when you're least able to deal with it? Some people are not born to be caretakers. And your daughter sounds like one of them.

GLORIA

Is that your advice, Doctor? Die alone. Less trouble for everyone?

DR. LEWITT

I wish I could help you. But I can't.

GLORIA

(Pleading)

All it means is a phone call to Santa Fe. One call. Here. I have her number.

(She desperately tries to hand him a slip of paper with the number.)

Take it! Please.

DR. LEWITT

(Firm, professional)

I'm sorry Mrs. Temple. It's a family matter that's outside my healing skills. You've asked me for time to finish your affairs. I've given you time. More time than most get with your condition. I have never lied to you. Or made promises I couldn't keep. The truth is. I've done *all* I can do.

(He turns away as she continues in her letter mode.)

MARCIE

Oh yes. You're so proud of your precious candor. You don't have the goddamned decency to lie to a dying woman. And you call it truth.

GLORIA

When I was young we always lied to the dying. It was part of the grand scheme of things – making people believe that there was hope. We did it with smiles and scolding, and stories and laughter.

MARCIE

Now we have advanced to a new kind of candor. One that uses truth as a club to kill all hope.

GLORIA

You goddamned technician, disguised as a healer. You think nothing of pushing tubes down my throat and drawing blood from my exhausted veins, long after it would do me any good.

MARCIE

That's easy for you to do.

GLORIA

But asking my daughter to stay with me until the end, that's beyond your calling.

MARCIE

So you leave me to die alone, with nothing but the truth, some painkillers and a tank of oxygen. Doctor, far better Marcie was here with me, hating me, than a cheerful nurse with her store-bought comfort. I want my child to hold me in this world while I am still in it. You can fill a textbook with what you know of lungs and their diseases, but you could not fill a scrap of paper with what you know of life.

> (*MARCIE puts down the letter, deeply moved by it. She stares absently, only called back to life by MRS. HOGAN. Quickly, she puts the letters back in drawer, unseen by the entering MRS. HOGAN and GLORIA.*)

MRS. HOGAN

We're back! He took us right away.

> (*MARCIE crosses to GLORIA, who looks up at her.*)

GLORIA

Thank God for that. That man has the worst magazines in his waiting room. Wrinkled old copies of *People* filled with stale scandals of film stars I never heard of. A wonder he has any patients.

MARCIE

Mother, I've thought over what you asked.
(*A long beat*)
I'll help with the foundation.

GLORIA

From Santa Fe?

MARCIE

No. I'll stay as long as you want me to be here with you.

GLORIA
(*Delighted*)

Thank you, Marcie. Thank you. What made you change your mind? Don't answer that! One shouldn't inspect a miracle too closely. It so easily falls apart. We'll have breakfast together in the morning. Now, I have Miss Himmelman coming in later, and I want her to give you a tour of the files. She's the perfect secretary except for her copper breath. Smells like she's been sucking pennies. Just don't get too close when she laughs. It's like she's making small change in a penny arcade. Fortunately, she rarely laughs.

MARCIE

Fair warning. Now, rest.

GLORIA
(*Through her difficulty in breathing*)

Soon. There's a conference with Stanley about some theatre company in San Francisco. They're doing *Girls of Laredo* with an all-male cast, and dumping the original Balanchine choreography in favor of some western line dancing. I've told Stanley to stop the production.

MARCIE

Why? It might be amusing.

GLORIA

Not to your father. He wanted his shows performed the way they were when first produced. You'll do that won't you?

MARCIE

Yes.

GLORIA

Well, now I can rest easy again.

MARCIE

Nonsense. Since you've never trusted my judgment, you'll watch me day and night, just so I don't screw up.

GLORIA
(Beginning to laugh)
Don't make me laugh. These days I can choke on my own joy.

> *(Her laughter brings on a coughing session. MARCIE, concerned, goes to help her, tripping over some tubes which she dislocates, removing the oxygen source from her mother's nostrils.)*

MARCIE
(Shouting)
Catherine – come quick!

> *(MRS. HOGAN waddles into the room and replaces the plastic clip in GLORIA's nostril that leads to the oxygen supply.)*

MRS. HOGAN
(Scolding GLORIA)
Well, we've done it now, haven't we? You take off that snorkel mask and think you can stay down in the deep chattering forever. Why it's time for our medicine and the early evening news. That always helps us rest before dinner, doesn't it?

GLORIA

Not yet. I need another moment with my daughter. .

MRS. HOGAN

Mrs. Temple, you must rest now.

GLORIA

Yes, yes, as soon as I go over my afternoon schedule with Marcie. I have Maurice, my hairdresser coming at three, and Mildred is coming round with some caftans from Bergdorf's. You know, they now sell the kind with Velcro fastening down the front for the stylishly disabled. You can slip in and out of it without dislodging a breathing tube, or drape it around a walker.

MARCIE

I thought you couldn't stand Millie.

GLORIA

I can't. But we've known each other forever and survival trumps affection at my age.

MARCIE

Mother, no more. Not another word.

GLORIA

Just four. Thank you my darling.

(*She gestures to MARCIE, who bends down and accepts her mother's kiss on the cheek.*)

MARCIE

Shall I fix you a cool pillow?

GLORIA

Thanks, but Mrs. Hogan's already done that. Mother always said it was unhealthy to sleep on a warm pillow. So she had the pillows turned by the servants at night. What an odd idea? And yet it's always stayed with me.

MARCIE

I know, I do the same myself. I turn my pillow when I wake in the night.

GLORIA

We're not so dissimilar then, are we?

MARCIE

I wouldn't go that far, Mother, except in the matter of cold pillows.

GLORIA

It's a start though, isn't it?

MARCIE

Yes. Rest now, please.

(*MRS. HOGAN takes GLORIA off. MARCIE turns on phonograph. We hear another song of Alex Temple being played. MRS. HOGAN returns.*)

MRS. HOGAN

Lovely tune. Must be your Daddy's, right?

MARCIE

Yes.

MRS. HOGAN

Ya don't hear anyone else's music in this house. God forbid I should play one of me old favorites, singin' someone else's song, and she'll ask me to turn it down.

MARCIE

John McCormack?

MRS. HOGAN

No. Elvis!

MARCIE

Catherine, this must be very hard for you.

MRS. HOGAN

Yes. And no. Some days she's a holy terror, but other times she couldn't be nicer. You know her.

MARCIE

She's lucky to have you.

MRS. HOGAN

And I'm blessed to have her. Thanks to her I've been able to put my children through some of the best schools in Ireland and start them off on such fine careers. Not a doorman or a barkeep in the lot. They are all praying for her, particular my eldest, Sister Mary Henry.

MARCIE

What will you do when she dies?

MRS. HOGAN

Why, go home to Ireland, of course. I miss my children like she misses you. She's always going on about your painting. She's so proud of you.

MARCIE

That's news.

MRS. HOGAN

Why? She loves you.

MARCIE

Needs me? Yes! Loves me? I'll have to take your word for that.

MRS. HOGAN

You can't have any doubts about it! You're all she has.

MARCIE

So she tells me.

> (*A beat. Holding back her emotion, seeking an occupation to distract herself*)

Worse than that, she's all *I have*. What will life be like when I have no one to disapprove of me *but myself?*

MRS. HOGAN

Do you have those letters of yours ready to mail?

MARCIE

Sorry. I got sidetracked. Can you wait another hour or so?

MRS. HOGAN

Of course I can. You take your time, dear.

> (*She exits. MARCIE puts on another recording, returns to the desk, begins to write, then finds another letter there, reads it.*)

MARCIE

My dear daughter, my Vivian. You broke my heart. I feel so betrayed. Pretentious word, betrayed. Queens are betrayed; the rest of us are simply fooled. And so you fooled me. During the blitz when I took you in as a war orphan, I had hoped that you would be a companion for my own daughter, Marcella, and that you could build a new life here. After a while I felt that we were the orphans and that you had taken us into your life as an act of charity. You seemed to be my natural child, thoughtful, well mannered, affectionate, respectful of others, a relief from Marcie in her perpetual turmoil.

GLORIA

Through you, Alex and I found a daughter who did not question our every motive, who did not challenge and threaten us with her anger, who did not sulk, complain, whine, and wheedle, who did not throw tantrums and catch colds as a sport. Now by eloping with your sister's husband, you have created a chasm between us that is so painful because it means another loss for me. I know it is absurd to ask, but I must.

GLORIA and MARCIE

Why Buddy?

MARCIE

I will grant him great natural charm, a clever mind, only diminished by a second rate moral sense. And those blue eyes of his – together with the rollicking laugh, the easy warmth – a heart breaker in my day. A heart breaker in any day. It was clear to me from the start that he married Marcie with his eye on the main chance; she would be his ticket out of a failing law practice into show business, and indeed, thanks to my husband, he became the producer of the Temple Blake films.

GLORIA

I suspected that Marcie would lose him to some film actress once he was firmly established, but I never dreamed that she would lose him to her sister.

MARCIE

You knew how much she cared for the man. He made her feel charming, loveable and desired. To do that, he had to be a con artist at the top of his game.

GLORIA

I thought you could see through him. But you chose merely to see him. Was the love making that good?

MARCIE and GLORIA

The secret meetings?

MARCIE

The risk of discovery?

GLORIA

Could anything hurt Marcie more than this elopement of a loved husband and a cherished sister, with you carrying the child she had wanted so much? So now you are asking me to find it in my heart to understand and forgive. Amazing question. Amazing answer. I do.

MARCIE

Odd, I could not know how much I loved you until you did this. The loss is terrible. And if I cannot stop loving you now, I suppose I never will. I wish I could stop loving you, since Marcie needs all my love now as she growls…

GLORIA

...and snaps...

MARCIE and GLORIA

...and roars...

MARCIE

...at me from her cage of bitterness. And you, in California, the Australia of the century, where we transport our charlatans and thieves in lieu of jail.

GLORIA

You are out of my will, but I cannot remove you from my life. I will never know if you were the scheming bitch Marcie says you were...

MARCIE

...or a woman victimized by the ruthless Buddy Sklar.

GLORIA

I may not forgive what you have done...

MARCIE and GLORIA

...but I understand it.

GLORIA

We can't really choose who we love, can we?

> (*Spotlight on VIVIAN who appears onstage as a figure in MARCIE's mind as the letters are read.*)

VIVIAN

Dear Momma Glory. What a gift you have given us, this sign of love, and forgiveness that it represents. When I sent you the birth announcement and the picture of *our own little Terry* all I hoped for was a word of congratulation, not an act of such generosity. The picture business is insecure at best, and the trust fund you set up for our little Terry will make certain that his schooling is provided for. Stanley said that you wanted us to tell no one about this, and of course we will honor your wishes. I understand your fears about Marcie finding out.

MARCIE and VIVIAN

God knows we never want to hurt her.

VIVIAN

I am sure you understand that. I dare not leave the house on Sunday evenings because I live for your Sunday phone calls. I've never really taken to L.A., although we have so many friends here and Buddy's career is flourishing. How I miss you and New York. We will keep sending you new pictures of Terry as you requested. We're planning a trip to the city in a few months, after postproduction on the new picture, and I'd love to introduce you to your adorable grandson at that time.

(MARCIE begins to flip through the notes as extracts from Vivian's letters are heard.)

VIVIAN

Momma Glory, Baby Terry celebrated his second birthday today. And your gift – so thoughtful – so generous. Darling, you'll be delighted to know that your grandson started nursery school this week. Alone among the toddlers, he didn't cry. I know he has your courage. Mother, Buddy and I loved seeing you in New York yesterday. We can't thank you enough for your generous help with the purchase of the new house in Beverly Hills. I know it's extravagant but, as Buddy says, one must look successful to stay successful out here. I wish you could visit us but I understand why you can't. We just hope that in time Marcie will come to forgive us. Terry so appreciated your High School graduation gift. He does nothing but wash and polish that new sports car day and night. Darling, how I loved my week in Essex. It was so good coming home again and spending those gorgeous early October days with you. Thanks again for Terry's college tuition check. You can't imagine what it costs to educate a child these days. I'm certain it's just a temporary dry spell in Buddy's work but... Thank you for helping us out. Thanks for the money...

MARCIE and VIVIAN

...the money... the money... the money... the money.

MARCIE

With much love from Buddy.

VIVIAN

Your deeply grateful...

MARCIE and VIVIAN

...and devoted daughter...

VIVIAN

Vivian.

MARCIE

Oh God, no! Mother, you did it. You fucking well did it! Goddamn bitch! You fooled me... again.

(The light dims on VIVIAN and holds on MARCIE as she stares at a baby photograph, then another picture. MARCIE begins to sob great gulping sobs, struggles to bring her emotions under control, and when she does so, she begins to breathe deeply in her effort to recover herself. She slams the surviving letters on to the desk, searches for envelopes, and she flips through the Rolodex and begins to address the envelopes in a driven, determined fashion. She takes out a roll of stamps and peels them back, methodically pressing them against the envelopes, then sealing each letter with her tongue, pounding each letter closed with her fist, rhythmic, savage, and crazed. Finally, she presses the buzzer under the desk with her foot. MRS. HOGAN appears.)

MARCIE

Sorry to disturb you, Mrs. Hogan, but I'm through with my letters. If you wouldn't mind mailing them now.

MRS. HOGAN

No trouble. I'll just throw on my coat. Now you rest, I've taken care of everything. She won't be getting up for dinner, if I know her she'll sleep through till morning. I've given her the painkiller, and I've just turned her pillow to the cool side. How that woman loves a cold pillow. If I let her have her way she'd store them in the fridge. We all have our strange ways, don't we?

MARCIE

Some stranger than others.

MRS. HOGAN

(Gently, to MARCIE)

You've had a long day, dear. You look so weary. Those airplanes get the best of me too. Lord, what a pile of letters you've got for me there. So many notes written in so short a time? You must write like a demon.

(MARCIE thrusts the letters at MRS. HOGAN.)

MARCIE

I do. They may only be bread and butter notes, but they matter.

MRS. HOGAN

A wonder you can write them feeling tired as you do. You're so like her, you are.

MARCIE

Well, if I've learned anything from my mother, it's not what we feel, but what we do that matters in this world.

LIGHTS OUT

ACT TWO

(The library. Two days later. MRS. HOGAN stomps through the room without speaking, picks up a bouquet of flowers from a vase, drops the flowers on the floor, replaces them with a fresh bunch, glowering at GLORIA, emitting a sound of disgust and not bothering to speak to MARCIE. She exits stiffly after this show of silent displeasure.)

GLORIA
(Hushed, conspiratorial)
What did I tell you? Mad? Right? Quite mad. An absolute raving loony.

MARCIE
I wouldn't go that far, Mother. But she does seem a bit out of sorts.

GLORIA
No. No, dear. *I'm* out of sorts. *She's* crazy. All day she has gone about grumbling under her breath, harrumphing and averting her eyes. She won't look at me. Why, this morning she jabbed my arm when she gave me my injection, and then, without so much as a "Good morning, Madam," she began speaking about her fine family in Cork being so accomplished.

MARCIE
(Suppressing a laugh)
Did she?

GLORIA
When she brought me my pills and juice, I swear she was mumbling that her boy was no cross-eyed bumpkin, but a Civil Engineer. And if that wasn't bad enough, someone called from my hairdresser, the great Monsieur Maurice, advising me that after years of serving me he will no longer be able to come to my suite to dress my hair. He suggests that I send for Supercuts. What the hell is Supercuts?

(MRS. HOGAN reenters the room, carrying the mail on a tray.)

MRS. HOGAN
Your mail, Madam.

GLORIA

Mrs. Hogan, Madam is a bit formal, given the years we've been together. I prefer Mrs. Temple, and I wouldn't even mind Gloria, if you think you can carry it off.

MRS. HOGAN

Yes, "Madam Gloria." And I prefer Mrs. Hogan to Bessie the cash cow.

GLORIA

What?

MRS. HOGAN

(With rising indignation)

Bumpkins? Louts? My Patrick is a state certified sanitary engineer. My Matthew is a chartered accountant. My Ruthie has her Master's Degree in child psychology, and my Mary is Sister Mary Henry of the Convent of the Sacred Heart, a Franciscan teaching order, and on her way towards becoming Mother Superior. And none of them ever drank a drop of whisky from a jar.

GLORIA

I'm sure they are all very sober and accomplished, but I don't quite understand what you are getting at?

MRS. HOGAN

I've brought the rest of your mail on your juice tray. I've lined up your medicines. I'll be going off to shop at the Gap in a few minutes to buy Christmas gifts for the bumpkins. Ah, and Doctor Lewitt's office called. He'll be out of town for your next appointment. He suggests you see his associate. Dr. Ravi Singh. So Punjab's on yer case.

(She exits.)

GLORIA

Thank you, Mrs. Hogan.

(To MARCIE)

Now am I right or am I right? Lord knows, anyone would go crazy who had to look after a demanding, ailing woman like me, but this is so quick. Darling, would you hand my glasses to me? I try to get the mail over early, you can't ever let it pile up. Look at what's stamped on this envelope.

(She studies one blue envelope, then another.)

GLORIA (Continued)

Return to sender. Dr. David Asher? He's been dead for years! Alex Temple?

(To MARCIE, with growing concern,
commanding)

Give me your arm. I have to go to my desk. Help me, Marcie. Now! What's that key doing there in the desk drawer? Oh, no!

(GLORIA, assisted by MARCIE, goes to her desk, seats herself, turns key in lock and opens the drawer.)

GLORIA

Gone. All gone. That wretched woman!

MARCIE

Something wrong, Mother?

GLORIA

Do you know what that lunatic has done?

MARCIE

No, Mother. What *has* that lunatic done?

GLORIA

She's mailed my letters.

MARCIE

Isn't that part of her job?

GLORIA

She went into my desk, read my old, unmailed letters that were never meant to be sent out into the world, or even to be seen by anyone but me. The dead won't be troubled by them but the living... the living. Oh Lord, they'll think I've gone gaga.

MARCIE

I'm not sure I follow you.

GLORIA

Years ago some quack told me to write out my angriest thoughts as letters, and then not mail them. It was supposed to help my migraines.

MARCIE

Did it?

GLORIA

Of course not. A crank cure, but I was so desperate I would have tried anything. Now it's clear that Mrs. Hogan has read these letters, particularly one addressed to her. Taking offense, she mailed the others to punish me. How could I be so careless, and she so vindictive?

MARCIE

Aren't you going to confront her with it?

GLORIA

If I was any good at confrontation, do you think I would have written those goddamned letters?

MARCIE

I think you must.

GLORIA

Must what?

MARCIE

Confront her.

(GLORIA presses buzzer under the desk as MARCIE rises to go.)

GLORIA

Of course I must. Stay. If she walks out on me now I'll need someone to help me get back to my bed. I don't want to die sitting up like Queen Elizabeth.

(MRS. HOGAN enters in her coat, looking angry and suspicious.)

MRS. HOGAN

Yes, Mrs. Temple? You called for me?

GLORIA

Mrs. Hogan. We can stop pretending. I know what you did.

MRS. HOGAN

And what was that, Madam?

GLORIA

Would you like to explain yourself?

MRS. HOGAN

Nothing for *me* to explain, Madam Gloria. I received your letter this morning, and it made very clear what you thought of me and my family. All these years I was deceived into thinking that you liked me.

GLORIA

But I do like you!

MRS. HOGAN

What kind of "like" sends a letter with such hurtful words in it? Bad enough what you said of me; me, who has been nothin' but yours to fetch and carry for a dozen years, but what you said of me children and me grandchildren; they who always remembered your birthday with a greeting card...

(Looking at MARCIE)

...which is more than some others have done. What you said of them – that went too far. You go about swanning it over the world like the great lady, but what you wrote to me was as hurtful as a tinker's curse.

GLORIA

You're making no sense. If I put down some private thoughts that offended you, I am sorry. But I didn't mail them, or ever intend that my angry words to be seen by you or anyone else.

MRS. HOGAN

Then you should have destroyed them, not leave them about like...like land mines ready to explode and destroy the innocent. All the grief they've caused.

GLORIA

You've brought this grief down on yourself. And me, I'm afraid. If you hadn't been snooping around my locked desk drawers you would never have seen the letter. And for you to mail the other letters was a very cruel and wanton act of retaliation. Nothing that I have ever done to you deserved that.

MRS. HOGAN
(Looking at MARCIE with suspicion)

No, I did not –

GLORIA

Mrs. Hogan, please don't lie to me.

MRS. HOGAN

I didn't rummage through your desk. And *I* didn't knowingly mail your letters. I got mine in the mail this morning. That's God's own truth.

GLORIA

Show me.

MRS. HOGAN

Here!

(She produces envelope and letter.)

GLORIA

Well, the stamp was properly cancelled. You say you never mailed the letters?

MRS. HOGAN

I didn't say that, Madam. I said I did, but *not knowingly.*

GLORIA

Yours, I take it, is the sleepwalker's defense?

MRS. HOGAN

I didn't know they were yours.

GLORIA

You confound me, Mrs. Hogan? Whose letters did you think you were mailing?

MRS. HOGAN

If you believe that I would do such a wicked thing as to give pain to an old woman, even a dreadful, insulting, arrogant old woman, you don't know me. I'm not to be upset! I can feel the pressure rising and my lungs filling up with fluid. If you are firing me, fire me now but I won't allow myself to be killed by you!

GLORIA

Thank you, Mrs. Hogan. I would like you to stay on, but if I have given such offense that it affects your health and your work, then you are free to go.

MRS. HOGAN

Oh, I'll stay on 'till you find a replacement. Were you jealous because I am loved? I am loved, Mrs. Temple. I am loved! If only by those louts, my grandchildren. Mrs. Temple. Mrs. Sklar.

(She exits.)

GLORIA

You know, the horror of it is I don't recall half the letters I kept in that desk. Fortunately, most of the recipients are dead. Only Mildred and my hairdresser and –

MARCIE

Don't you want to know why she mailed them?

GLORIA

I do know!

MARCIE

Do you?

GLORIA

I've put a terrible burden on her. I was far too selfish when I fired the night nurse. I didn't want anyone else touching me, meddling in my life; she knew all my habits. And she never once complained. Mind you, I pay her a small fortune to take care of me. And for that I exhausted her mind and her patience. I drove her mad with my demands. Lucky she didn't kill me.

MARCIE

I'm sure you exaggerate.

GLORIA

(Turning aside as she speaks)

No! Sometimes I soil my bed in the night as I sleep. She washes my bottom like a baby, and she makes light of it. Dusting me with corn starch. Pretending it never happened. Poor Mrs. Hogan. She must have been nosing around my desk out of sheer boredom. Then she found some old un-mailed letters. One of them was quite critical of her. So she mailed all of them to hurt me as I had hurt her.

MARCIE

You don't want to question her further? Get to the bottom of it?

GLORIA

That is the bottom of it. I am the bottom of it.

MARCIE

You'd trust her to give you your medications?

GLORIA

What do I risk? If she keeps me alive she's giving me more time to finish my work here. If she kills me, she takes me out of my pain. But she'll keep me alive. It's the only thing she knows how to do.

MARCIE

You are being facetious, but I know it must upset you terribly.

GLORIA

It does. I don't like to feel pain or to give pain. And clearly I do.

MARCIE

Do? Do? Do what?

GLORIA

Give it. Pain. I've given a great deal of it to you, haven't I? Always offering you advice you didn't want, and voicing opinions you didn't care to hear.

MARCIE

Yes, but I've never been easy.

GLORIA

Just as well. Terry was easy...and what good did it do him?

MARCIE

Vivian was easy too.

GLORIA

You weren't the only one betrayed there.

MARCIE

You mean fooled?

GLORIA

Yes. Fooled.

(*The TELEPHONE rings.*)

MARCIE

Mildred? Yes, it's Marcie. I arrived on Tuesday. I'll tell her. Milly Wurtz is here. In the lobby. Do you want to see her?

GLORIA

No. Tell her I'm tired. I'm resting.

MARCIE

I'm sorry Mildred, mother's resting.
(*To GLORIA*)
She says she won't disturb you. She wants to drop something off.

GLORIA

God knows what I wrote to her years ago. I can't recall.

MARCIE

Shall I tell her you won't see her?

GLORIA

Yes. But let her come up. Just see what she wants.

MARCIE

Come up if you like, but Mother can't see you. She's resting.
(To GLORIA)
Milly's coming.

GLORIA

How did she sound?

MARCIE

Like Milly. Ruthlessly cheerful.

GLORIA

Then it must be all right. Remember, I'm sleeping. I just took a pill.

MARCIE

I don't lie very well.

GLORIA

I wouldn't be so proud of that. It's moral boasting. Try.

(GLORIA lowers her head, feigning sleep. MILDRED, a small, flamboyant woman, one arm in a sling, carrying a three pronged aluminum walker which she plants on the floor and uses as a hat rack, as MARCIE helps her off with her coat.)

MILDRED

Hello Marcie.

MARCIE

Please, speak softly. Mother took a pill and went out like a light.

(MILDRED pulls MARCIE down to kiss her.)

MILDRED
(Louder)

So I see. Sweetie, you haven't changed a bit since I last saw you. Was it really two years ago?

MARCIE

Is that good or bad, Milly?

MILDRED

Good. The nice thing about being plain is you don't age as much as the great beauties. Look at the Duchess of Windsor. Face like a Japanese demon in a Noh play. Looked no worse when she was old than when silly Edward met her. And me? Never much to look at but now I can pass for a handsome seventy on a good day. But your mother. All that beauty drying up and blowing away under your eyes like dandelion fluff. How's she doing?

MARCIE

About the same.

MILDRED

And how is your life in Santa Fe! I adore Santa Fe.

MARCIE

How original. Are you well?

(MILDRED hands Bergdorf's shopping bag to MARCIE.)

MILDRED

Well? Well, I sprained my wrist the other day simply flushing a toilet. Believe me, this sling is no fashion accessory. I'm always breaking or spraining something nowadays. The arthritis pain in my knee forces me to take cortisone and that puffs up my face and keeps the wrinkles at bay.

MARCIE

That's good.

MILDRED

No, it eats away the lining of my stomach, so I don't really digest a meal anymore. The medication I take for my stomach gives me the runs, so I plan my day so that I'm never too far from a bathroom. At least it keeps me thin.

MARCIE

How's your son Andy?

MILDRED

(Completely disinterested in him,
moving ahead)

My glaucoma is so bad that I can hardly read anymore. My housekeeper gets me these large print books out of the library, and I feel like I'm back in grammar school. Only the text has changed from "See Jane Run" to "See Milly Die."

MARCIE

And your daughter?

MILDRED

*(Waving off the question as she spies the
back of her own hand)*

I've got hands like a speckled hen, and spots on my face that would
be the envy of any breeder of Springer Spaniels. I don't sleep more
than three hours a night, but for my age, I suppose I'd have to say *I'm
absolutely wonderful.*

MARCIE

I'll tell her you were here when she gets up. Does she owe you
anything for this?

MILDRED

Yes, but she's good for it. Besides, I mean to speak with her. Marcie. I
lied about just dropping it off. Don't try to stop me. Touch me and I
break.

*(She walks over to GLORIA, waves her hand in front of her closed
eyes.)*

MILDRED

Those lashes are fluttering. You're not sleeping, Sweetie. And I'm not
fooled.

GLORIA

Milly, this is a poor time. Marcie and I have business between us.

MILDRED

And so do we, Gloria. I know my visits can annoy you, but –

GLORIA

They don't. They give me such pleasure when I see you go.

MILDRED

Sickness hasn't tamed that tongue.

GLORIA

If you're here about some letter, I won't apologize. Mrs. Hogan took it
on herself to mail some old letters, written in anger that I never
intended to mail.

MILDRED

I figured it was something like that. None the less, I was quite hurt.

GLORIA

I'm sorry Milly. But you must go. I'm not myself.

MILDRED

Who is?

(She unwraps caftan as she speaks and spreads it over GLORIA.)

Blue. You always looked your best in blue. Very few people do, you know. Me. I need red just to look alive these days. There are some things we'd better clear up now. Marcie, stay. There's no point in hiding anything from you.

MARCIE

I wouldn't think of leaving now.

MILDRED

Well, say this for that letter. It shows I was wrong about you. You were no silently suffering wife.

GLORIA

Fine. And you were no friend, just a slut who had only one thing to offer a man.

MILDRED

Slut? Nonsense. I was avant-garde.

GLORIA

What?

MILDRED

A little ahead of my time. I was plain, and I slept with boys. You thought it was to make myself popular. That was just a side benefit. I liked the good feelings of sex. So I fucked while you stayed pure and smoked your gold tipped Dunhills. And I was a scandal and you were the Lady Gloria. Only I still get around by myself while you lie there hooked up to hideous plastic tubes, struggling for every breath through that nasal thingamajig. Proves that fucking beats smoking any day of the week.

GLORIA

All right, you've had your say, now –

MILDRED

And about my hairdos. You are no one to talk. Yes. I always had mine cut to suit the fashion of the times. But you wore yours piled up high on your head like a goddamned Gibson Girl with her noble forehead. I suppose it enhanced your virginal image, and Alex liked it.

(To MARCIE)

It's amazing how your mother remained a virgin through two childbirths and one miscarriage. If you didn't look so like your father, Marcie, I'd swear you were the offspring of your Holy Mother and the Holy Ghost.

(MARCIE laughs.)

And as far as my sleeping with Alex that summer, which is, I suppose, what provoked you to write that letter, I have always regretted it. I didn't really want to. Alex was never my type. Don't much care for brainy, talented men with short, fat fadoodles. All of my husbands were rich, dumb, and well hung; inheritors of their family fortunes, not geniuses who came up from the streets. And I adored them all, the darling dodos. When they died all of them left me their money. Not a goddamned foundation dropper in the bunch.

(Gently)

Gloria, it was an old thing with Alex and me.

GLORIA

When did it begin?

MILDRED

Twenty-nine... thirty. I can't recall.

GLORIA

(Astonished)

But I started dating him in twenty-nine!

MILDRED

Then it was twenty-nine.

GLORIA

That's impossible. He was wildly in love with me.

MILDRED

Yes, he was. After a date with you he would call me and arrange for a tryst in some downtown hotel. No Mr. and Mrs. Smith for Alex. When we registered it was Mister and Mrs. Gregory Pappas or Renaldo DiMaria, or some marvelous ethnic married name full of sunlight and grape-leaves. Leave it to Alex. He always put a lot of thought into cheating on you. He considered you an angel, a saint, and he loved you dearly. Because of me he never knew what a cunning piece of work you were, until he married you. You should have thanked me. Without my being such an obliging creature, he might have wised up and married some hot-blooded kid from the chorus.

GLORIA

And you schemed to get him back. So years later –

MILDRED

No. After you were married we never got together again privately. Not until we met by chance at the Colony that summer. You've got to trust me on this. I didn't call him, he phoned me.

GLORIA

Did he, really?

MILDRED

I was between husbands, and what the hell, more than a little randy. I didn't want to do it in your bed, but it gave him an extra thrill. As far as your finding that earring, I didn't lose it deliberately. I know I should have had my ears pierced when you did, but unlike you I'm such a coward. So I was condemned to wear those awful screw-on numbers. Alex must have nibbled it loose. Maybe it just fell off when I was going down on him. Or as you noted so eloquently, when I "pioneered fellatio" on the Upper East Side. I'm amazed my poor lobe wasn't shaken off with that earring.

GLORIA

I don't believe this. You are saying this to get back at me for that letter.

MILDRED

I don't want revenge. I just want to set the record straight. Darling, I wasn't the first, or the last.

GLORIA

Old news. Actresses. Girls from the chorus. One expected that. It's routine for men working on a show on the road to have such affairs. Why they are hardly affairs. Just interludes. But you were my friend, my closest friend.

MILDRED

And so I am. I never told a soul about Alex. Not like Barbara Blount. She blabbed all over town about herself and Alex.

GLORIA

Barbara? Tommy Blount's wife?

MILDRED

Yes. But that's perfectly understandable. Everyone knew that Tommy was queer. But a damned fine director, wasn't he? She was on the plane with Alex when he flew out to Hollywood to work on some film score for something Tommy was directing at MGM. And Evelyn Venable? Why, you two were so close. You did all your charity work together, always gabbing on the phone. I was jealous of all that garrulous goodness. Take it from me, she was closer still with Alex.

GLORIA

Why do you tell me this? They're all dead and can't speak for themselves. So why should I believe you?

MILDRED

Because you do.

GLORIA

You're disgusting!

MILDRED

I do hope so. It was always the centerpiece of my charm.

GLORIA

Please, get out and take that hideous caftan with you. I hate the color. I hate the pattern. I hate the gold. Most of all, I hate you.

MILDRED

I'm sorry, dear. You don't hate me and I won't stop caring about you. My God, we are the only ones left who knew each other when we were young. We shared so many laughs and memories, what difference does it make that I once shared your husband? Marcie, tell her I love her. What happened with your father was so long ago, she shouldn't carry on about it. You will survive this, my dear. What does not kill us makes us stronger.

GLORIA

Where did you learn that nonsense?

MARCIE

It's Nietzsche, Mother.

GLORIA

Some Nazi nonsense.

MILDRED

Never read 'em. I first came across it on a goddamned needlework pillow. My son Andy sent it to me for my last birthday. Feel better, Gloria. Marcie, do stay with her as long as you can. She needs you now. Don't worry, I'll bring the goddamned caftan back to Bergdorf's. Keeps me fit. If they had an Olympics for shopping and returning, I'd get the gold. Gloria, I'll call you soon. Marcie, I love your hair color. It's so courageous.

(*She exits.*)

GLORIA

Well, she's right about one thing. I do need you now. I'm so glad you're here. Now I'll have all kinds of wonderful surprises.

MARCIE

Wonderful?

GLORIA

Why, you're being here. Helping me get through this. We've reversed roles, haven't we?

MARCIE

I wouldn't have it any other way, Mother.

(The TELEPHONE rings again. MARCIE looks at it and lets it ring.)

GLORIA

For God's sake, answer it.

MARCIE
(Answering phone)
Yes. No. I'll have to see.
(To GLORIA)
It's the Smithsonian man. He wants to see you. Wants isn't quite it. Demands an audience is more like it.

GLORIA

We didn't have an appointment until next week.

MARCIE

He says he just received your letter.

GLORIA

Tell him I'll see him. We don't want this nonsense to affect Daddy's exhibition.

MARCIE

Of course we don't.
(To PARKER-BENTON)
Come up. Yes, now.

GLORIA

I know exactly what I wrote. It wasn't too long ago. I accused him of stealing a rehearsal photo of *The Girl Said Yes*. Couldn't find it after one of our meetings.

MARCIE

What was so special about it?

GLORIA

Nothing, really. The usual rehearsal stuff. Daddy playing at the rehearsal piano with an unlit cigarette dangling from his mouth, the ingénue hanging over him adorningly, ready to strike a match if he wanted it. And him looking up at her with – with whatever it is that men look at pretty girls with. The minute Parker-Benton saw it I watched those beady eyes grow enormous with curatorial lust.

(The DOOR BELL rings.)

GLORIA

Show him in.

(*PARKER-BENTON bursts into the room holding up letter and photograph.*)

MR. PARKER-BENTON

Why, Mrs. Temple? Why?

GLORIA

Enough that it's true, isn't it?

MR. PARKER-BENTON

But it's not! I never stole this picture. You lent it to me for the exhibition.

GLORIA

Impossible.

MR. PARKER-BENTON

How can you say that? You gave me so many photos of your husband in rehearsal.

GLORIA

Not that picture. Not that show. You slipped it in with the others while I was looking elsewhere.

MR. PARKER-BENTON

No! You are mistaken.

GLORIA

I would never have made such a mistake. That was a private picture. Now give it here!

(*He hands the photograph over to her reluctantly.*)

MR. PARKER-BENTON

It was only a rehearsal photograph, nothing private about it.

GLORIA
(*Allowing herself a long look at the picture*)

You do know that Benita Heywood was my husband's mistress during the run of that show?

MR. PARKER-BENTON

I'd heard rumors of course, but –

GLORIA

It was a somewhat longer affair than most of Alec's diversions. There was a time when I feared he might leave me for her. A groundless fear, but it caused me great pain. There was no way I would have given you that photo to put on public display. No way.

MR. PARKER-BENTON

Mrs. Temple, we're living in a new world. Don't you think we should show the whole man? The human behind the lovely songs?

GLORIA

And how do we do that? Hang his sordid little affairs up there in the Smithsonian beside the Spirit of St. Louis for everyone to gape at? Is that your idea of honoring him? No! You told me that this exhibition was about his contribution to American music. If it strays from that path I will recall all the materials I lent to the museum and you can expect nothing further from me. Including his personal papers. Yes, yes, I was planning to will them to your organization, with you as custodian together with my authorization for you to write his biography. Now, are you prepared to honor my husband as the great artist he was? Or will you degrade him and his great accomplishments by shining a follow spot on his restless penis.

MR. PARKER-BENTON

I would never –

GLORIA

Thank you, I take you at your word. We will meet again next week, and God willing, get through 1939. And thank you for returning the photograph. It's number three-seven-four-two, right?

(She turns it over to check number on back.)

Right! Don't apologize. What's a little theft? It just makes you more human. I look forward to our next conversation.

MR. PARKER-BENTON

(Shaken)

As do I!

(He holds out his hand, but she waves him off without taking it. As he departs she allows herself to show her exhaustion.)

MARCIE

You're good. First the stick, then the carrot. Actually, you turn the carrot into a stick. How do you do it? Where do you find the strength?

GLORIA

It's there. Just know what you want, and don't give in until it's yours.

MARCIE

Did you really think he would leave you for that girl?

GLORIA

Yes. At the time I did. I was so hurt, so angry. Hated him. Hated her. Worse. Hated me. But we weathered it. Told him we need never talk of this again as long as he acted with discretion in the future and he stopped seeing button eyes immediately. At the end of the day, the comfort of a well-kept home was too hard for him to abandon.

MARCIE

You never quit, do you?

GLORIA

I'll take that as a compliment.

MARCIE

Take it any way you like. But take it and rest. You look exhausted.

GLORIA

I am. It isn't every day one has to stand up to a national museum.
(Staring at the photograph)
I must replace this in the file now.

(She exits the library.)

MARCIE

I'll still be here when you get up, trust me on that.

(MRS. HOGAN enters removing her own hat and coat in the foyer.)

MARCIE

No luck at the Gap.

MRS. HOGAN

Didn't go. Went to church. Prayed for guidance. In my confession I asked the Father if I should take on the guilt of another in order to spare an old woman. He said that only Christ could take on the sins of others;

that we poor sinners had to deal with our own, not go about adding others to our mortal pile. So I'm gonna tell her if you don't.

MARCIE

Tell her? What?

MRS. HOGAN

That you gave me those dreadful letters to mail.

MARCIE

You'll break her heart.

MRS. HOGAN

You should have thought of that before.

MARCIE

Break it.

MRS. HOGAN

What?

MARCIE

I said break it. It may well kill her. Then you can be my accomplice. You'll have spared me the pain of a confession. I hand you the gun, you will pull the trigger, so to speak.

MRS. HOGAN

You can't be that wicked.

MARCIE

I don't know what you mean by that.

MRS. HOGAN

You hate her so much? She, who loves you so.

MARCIE

Mrs. Hogan, I don't hate her... so much. And she doesn't love me... so. But we both pretend we do. And that's the sad sadness of it.

MRS. HOGAN

Well, if you want her to know, you'll have to tell her. No, I will not do it to her. She has enough to do now. Dyin' is such hard work. There's no trainin' for it. Some, I dare say, do it better than others, with a little love to ease the way. I look at the pair of you and your Punch and Judy show and ask myself why? Perhaps it's divine justice. Why else would such a mother have such a daughter? Divine justice, that's what it is. But let her answer to the Almighty for her faults. Not to me, Mrs. Sklar. And certainly not to *you*. Goodnight.

> *(MARCIE stands in silence, says nothing. MRS. HOGAN exits. The TELEPHONE rings. MARCIE stands there as it rings, letting it ring until the answering machine picks it up.)*

GLORIA'S VOICE
(On answering machine)

You've reached Lehigh 5-3894. Sorry I'm not able to take your call. Please leave your name and number at the tone and I'll get back to you.

VIVIAN'S VOICE (on machine)

Momma Glory, its Viv. I've been so worried. I didn't hear from you on Sunday and today, I got this old letter in the mail. You may have written it in anger years ago, but you would never mail it now – in the midst of all our troubles. It must be some dreadful mistake. I hate to ask for your help now but rehab for Terry costs a small fortune. He was okay for a while. Then, last week, we discovered that he was using again. So we put him in this very expensive center in Arizona. We can't keep him there more than a week or two. The money's gone. And the house is so mortgaged we can't squeeze another cent out of it. You know Buddy hasn't made a picture in five years. He keeps saying it will all change soon, that he has this film in development at Warners, ready to go. Means nothing. Won't happen. Every valet who parks your car in this town claims he has a film in development at some studio. At least they have their tips to support their illusions. I didn't want to bother you again, knowing how ill you've been, but your grandson needs your help desperately. I've no one to turn to but you. Mother, please have Stanley wire some money into my account now.

MARCIE
(Picking up the phone and speaking into it.)

Sorry lady, banking hours are over. We're closed for the day.

VIVIAN'S VOICE

What? Marcie? Marcie!

MARCIE

Home for the holidays! So, you got mother's greeting card?

VIVIAN'S VOICE
(Accusing)

You sent that awful letter! You forged her handwriting and –

MARCIE
(In the voice of a Quiz Show host,
buzzer noises and all)

Vivian Sklar, housewife and mother from Beverly Hills California, a good guess but you have just missed winning the grand prize on the Gloria Temple Show. The correct answer is: Momma wrote it years ago, Marcie just found it and mailed it.

VIVIAN'S VOICE

Does she know what you've done?

MARCIE

No. She thinks Mrs. Hogan went wild and mailed all the angry letters.

VIVIAN'S VOICE

There were more letters?

MARCIE

Enough.

VIVIAN'S VOICE

Don't tell her you mailed them. Please. Don't. She's so frail you can't –

MARCIE

So frail? And yet you dump your ton of garbage on her head; your pathetic husband, your drugged out son, and your own wretched life. All for her to cure with Temple love and Temple money.

VIVIAN'S VOICE

You've no idea of what I'm going through. There's nothing worse than losing your child when he's still alive.

MARCIE

I'm afraid I don't know. Mine died before he lived. You remember my late miscarriage? Was that when you started in with Buddy?

VIVIAN'S VOICE

I'm so sorry.

MARCIE

For what you've done to me? Or to yourself? We know about Buddy and the boy, but what about you, Viv? How do you get through your days? Of course, *you* garden and you worry. And you visit with your family therapist, hoping something you did made Terry what he is *so you* can undo it. He was supposed to go to Harvard, and now he's flunking rehab.

VIVIAN'S VOICE

Marcie, if it gives you comfort, I've never felt worse in my life.

MARCIE

Look on the bright side, Viv. If Buddy was prospering, he'd probably have left you for another woman. You're long past your expiration date. Only his failure keeps you together. Either way, it must be hell. Speaking of hell, mother has arrived.

(GLORIA enters the room, holding on to a walker.)

GLORIA

Who is that?

MARCIE

Mrs. Miniver.

GLORIA

Who?

MARCIE

Hollywood Viv? Want to talk to her?

GLORIA
(Longing to take phone, but deciding against it)

No. Not now. I'll call her later.

MARCIE

She'll call you later. Lovely chatting with you.

(She hangs up the receiver.)

GLORIA

What did she want?

MARCIE

Money. Her boy is in trouble, Buddy's broke, and she's desperate.

GLORIA

Old news. Sad news. Never stops.

(A long beat as she stares at MARCIE)

I must tell Stanley to send her something tomorrow. I hope you weren't too cruel.

(A beat)

Don't tell me. I'd rather not know what you said. You do have an infinite capacity for mischief.

MARCIE

You really don't know what she did to my life?

GLORIA

Yes, I do. She saved you from Buddy Sklar.

MARCIE

What?

GLORIA

She took on the burden of being his wife. And you went on to become a fine painter in a place you love. You survived, Marcie, and in your own way, you thrived. But Vivian? How awful it must have been for her to get my letter, when she was in such despair. Did it give you great pleasure to send it?

MARCIE

So now you accuse me of mailing the letters? How like you to think the worst of me.

GLORIA

Stop it Marcie! It had your signature touch. I didn't want to think you could do anything so cruel. That you hated me so much.

MARCIE

I don't.

GLORIA

Please. I may have lapses in memory, but not in judgment.
(Breaking for the first time)
Why?

MARCIE

How can you ask that? You invited back into your life the very people who wrecked mine. Did you ever think what that would mean to me? You sanctioned what they did to me!

GLORIA

I am so alone since Daddy died. I can't afford to lose another person I love.

MARCIE

Meaning Vivian? Not me! I am quite losable, right Mother? Well, consider me lost.

GLORIA

I need you both. You most of all.

MARCIE

It isn't me you want. It's someone who will protect Daddy's work with her life. Because she has no other life. And why don't I have another life? Ask yourself that?

GLORIA

(Enraged)
If you have no other life – that was your doing. Not mine. You're a middle aged woman. Not some rebellious child I can't control. You have enough money from the family trust to live any way you wish. I thought by this time you would take responsibility for all the bad and the good that has happened to you. But no! You prefer to whine about the past and play cruel tricks... childish tricks.

MARCIE

You'd say anything to win your case against me.

GLORIA

Won't you ever learn? Every time you rage against me or Daddy, you rage against yourself. You have turned my dying into a drama about your goddamned wasted life.

MARCIE

I didn't write those letters. I didn't express my loathing for you.

GLORIA

If I mentioned your storms and your disturbances – it was just a weather report of the day. It's clear that I failed you as a mother. I can't undo that. True, I wasn't much for coddling and compliments, we didn't do that then, but it didn't mean that I –

MARCIE

You're lying! You had enough soft words for Vivian.

GLORIA

She wasn't mine. She was a foreign child, an orphan who depended upon me.

MARCIE

And me? Didn't I depend on you?

GLORIA

No! You depended on your rage to get you through the day. Hating me has been your real career, hasn't it? The painting is just your hobby. A pastime. Well, I hope all that hating has given you some pleasure; otherwise it was just wasted pain.

MARCIE

Even in your angry letter you cry out to her, your "true" daughter" as she runs off with my husband!

GLORIA

I never forgave her for that. She betrayed my trust.

MARCIE

Your trust? That's what it was all about. You! My feelings didn't matter. Of course feelings don't matter, do they? It's only our actions that count. Well, you acted on your feelings, goddamn it. You went back into their life.

GLORIA

I am not responsible for Buddy Sklar not loving you.

MARCIE

But he did love me.

GLORIA

You delude yourself.

MARCIE

If he didn't love me, I would have known that.

GLORIA

How? You were so young. You had no experience of life.

MARCIE

Thanks to you, I always knew what it was like *not to be loved*. What did you see when you looked at me? A female version of Daddy, a sturdy little peasant out of Rivington Street, with blunt fingers and coarse, unmanageable hair, and worst of all, an insolent way of talking back to you. I knew you couldn't love me, just as I knew that, Buddy Sklar did. He loved my impertinent wit, he loved my paintings, he loved my rebellion, and he loved my fortune, but most of all, he loved my loving him. Buddy Sklar loved me. *Just not enough.*

(MARCIE weeps; she covers her face. GLORIA reaches out to her but MARCIE pulls away.)

GLORIA

Marcie – I never meant to –

MARCIE

Mother, shall I dial Vivian for you? I imagine she'd jump at the chance to run the Foundation now. It's okay. From now on I don't care what you do.

GLORIA

No. Nothing has changed.

MARCIE

I don't believe that.

GLORIA

Your father wanted you to take over and I am here to see that his wishes are carried out. He found you intelligent and up to the task. He never cared for Vivian.

MARCIE

When did Daddy tell you that?

GLORIA

He didn't have to. I knew his mind as well as my own. We were married forever.

MARCIE

Yes, a wonderful marriage.

GLORIA

It was the best I ever knew. He needed me.

MARCIE

For what?

GLORIA

For everything!

MARCIE

Not for sex, not for money, not for praise, not for comfort. He had the admiration of the world. Just what did he need from you?

GLORIA

I was. . . I was. . . his muse. We were one perfect pair. I made his life possible. I absorbed all the shocks so that he could work in peace. I carried on the just causes, raised the children, gave the dinner parties, furnished the houses, kept the bores at bay and brought the clever to the table. I was the keeper of the peace. Until Terry's death.

MARCIE

How could you live with someone who drove your son to his death?

GLORIA

How do I know it wasn't an accident! Life is nothing but accidents and misadventures, people falling in front of trains, people falling from windows, people falling out of love… falling into old age and sickness and death. Gravity is the enemy.

(*A long beat*)

Oh, Marcie, Daddy's life was of no importance to anyone but us. At the end, there is only his music. Without his music…without him… I was just a lost lady with bad headaches and a very long day. .

MARCIE

So you forgave him? Again and again and again. I don't know that I can.

GLORIA

He was never cruel to you.

MARCIE

He was worse than cruel. He was indifferent.

GLORIA

I know he loved you as much as he loved anyone, but the songs came first. Marcie, I'll soon be gone. Like it or not, you will do what you must. You'll do what's right for Daddy.

MARCIE

Whatever that is.
(Savagely)
Screw him! But Lord, spare the music.

GLORIA

One thing is sure. *You'll* never have a migraine, my darling. You want an apology for my grievous faults, fine, I apologize.

MARCIE

You don't mean it.

GLORIA

You're goddamned right I don't! You're getting much more than an apology. You get the songs and the fortune they made. The fortune they make. And that gives you the power to do some good in this world. A new life. So use it carefully.

MARCIE

What shall you do about Mrs. Hogan?

GLORIA

Nothing. When she considers her pension to be, and her Christian duty to forgive the sinner, she'll soon be her old tiresome, adoring self. Why are we always loved by the wrong people?

MARCIE

Worse. Why do we always love the wrong people?

GLORIA

Buddy Sklar?

MARCIE

No, I meant you.

(A beat)

Me, loving you. I do, you know. It would be so easy if I didn't.

GLORIA

If that's a lie – thank you. If it's the truth – forgive me.

(GLORIA lets out a loud, involuntary sob of grief.)

MARCIE

(Ruefully)

What a pair we are.

GLORIA

But it was worth it… just to have you with me, now. I was so lonely, Marcie. Memories can make such bad company. They often come uninvited, overstay their welcome and leave a mess behind.

(Back in the moment)

What do you plan to do? Go back to New Mexico tomorrow and spare yourself my tiresome death scene. I don't blame you. I'd avoid it myself, if I wasn't forced to attend it.

MARCIE

No. Mother, I'll stay with you to the end.

GLORIA

You're not Mrs. Hogan. You don't have to.

MARCIE

I want to. You saw me into the world. I'll see you out of it. But I won't run the Foundation. Not here. Not anywhere. Trust me on that. I'm going back to New Mexico, to live on my terms. Not yours. Not Daddy's. With nobody's shadow but my own.

GLORIA

You set yourself quite a task. The greater the parent, the deeper the shadow. His will find you, even in Santa Fe. So I've lost you.

MARCIE

Nobody's lost. We've simply called a truce.

GLORIA

A lull in the battle.

MARCIE

A hiatus between storms.

GLORIA

A *caesura* within the lines. Darling, I'd like to hear that old recording of Daddy's. I get so thirsty at night. I need a drink of music before I go to bed.

> *(MARCIE starts the record. They stand there listening to it, separate and alone.)*

Enough. It's time for the ten o'clock news. It's a comfort, you know. No matter how bad we feel, the world is always in worse shape than we are. Call Mrs. Hogan if you like.

MARCIE

No. I'll take you there myself. And I'll turn your pillow to the cold side, so you can sleep through the night.

> *(They walk slowly towards the bedroom as the LIGHTS FADE and the music plays on.)*

END OF PLAY

BUDAPEST

BUDAPEST

A New Play
by Sherman Yellen

It is 1964 in New York City and twenty-somethings Arnie and Robb
attend the funeral of a once famous Austrian actor hoping to meet
celebrities who might help jumpstart their screenwriting careers. Here
they meet Minna, a beautiful survivor of her horrific European past
who invites them into her life with consequences that change them
all. *Budapest* is a dark comedy, a modern *Camille*, and a story of love
and betrayal, recreating the fragile world of theatre émigrés in New
York City in the decades following World War II.

All the events take place in New York City.

ACT ONE

Scene 1: Ante room of the Riverside Chapel,
Amsterdam Avenue. April 1964.

Scene 2: Minna's walkup apartment on the
Upper West Side. One hour later.

Scene 3: Minna's apartment. Six months later.

ACT TWO

Minna's apartment

Scene 1: Three months later.

Scene 2: One year later.

Scene 3: One year later.

CHARACTERS

ROBB RHINEHARDT, a glib, charming, ambitious child of Hollywood, 24

ARNIE FORMAN, his roommate, a fledgling screenwriter, 24.

KLOTTIE BENEDICKS, the widow of a great Austrian actor, emotional, outrageous, 50.

MINNA BENEDICKS, a beautiful, intelligent survivor, 40s.

BRIGITTA, a fading German film star, glamorous and self-serving, 50

RABBI; SAM FORMAN (Arnie's father); and the voice of TOCHTIN.

ACT ONE

Scene One

(Two young men, ARNIE FORMAN and ROBB RHINEHARDT, stand at the entrance to the chapel.)

ARNIE

Are you sure?

ROBB

Sure I'm sure.

ARNIE

It feels wrong. It feels –

ROBB

Get over it, Arn. Stop trying to pass your nerves off as scruples.

ARNIE

The last time I felt this guilty I was a kid sneaking into the Loewe's Grand in Trenton – without paying. But this is no movie. It's real grief. Somebody's goddamned pain.

ROBB
(Forging ahead)
Trust me. Klottie will remember Gundi. I think she might even have had an affair with Gundi in Berlin. These people are like one big family.

ARNIE

With a lot of incest! Maybe she'll think *you* belong here. But me? What am I?

ROBB

The best friend of the stepson of a man who knew her husband in Europe before the war.

ARNIE

We didn't know him! This kind of opportunism is shameful shit.

ROBB

Is that why you think I came here? Opportunism? Did you ever think that I might love these old refugees and revere their art? Honor their ordeals.

(A beat)

And still be an opportunist!

(ARNIE laughs.)

Maybe I am, but if you were a real friend you'd call it pragmatism. What's wrong with you, anyway?

ARNIE

We're the only ones here under fifty.

ROBB

So? We'll stand out. She'll notice us when she arrives.

ARNIE

You really think *she's* coming?

ROBB

Of course she's coming.

ARNIE

How can you be sure?

ROBB

They were great friends in Berlin. Brigitta will be here. She's loyal to a fault.

(Two women in black enter, the attractive younger one, MINNA, supporting the older one, KLOTTIE.)

ROBB (Continued)

There's Klottie. Come on. Teeth do your stuff.

(He smiles a dazzling smile as they approach KLOTTIE the widow Benedicks arguing with her sister-in-law, MINNA. MINNA is in her middle forties, a strikingly beautiful woman.)

KLOTTIE

How could you let me do this, Minna? How could I know? I'm not Jewish. Now this Rabbi tells me that cremation is not for Jews.

MINNA

Who cares what that Rabbi says? Anton was a Jew, yes. But he was an actor first. He would never have forgiven us if we had him laid out in an open casket.

KLOTTIE

You're right, of course. And to think we will never again see him seated at a dressing table, putting on another incredible nose.

(KLOTTIE begins to weep. MINNA places a comforting arm around KLOTTIE, patting her back.)

MINNA

There... there.

KLOTTIE

(She clutches her heart and pounds it with her fist.)

No. Here. Here.

ROBB

(Turning to KLOTTIE)

Madam Benedicks? Klottie? Robb Rhinehardt. And Arnie Forman.

KLOTTIE

(Turning to ARNIE)

Yes?

ARNIE

I'm... I'm so sorry.

KLOTTIE

Why? You didn't kill Anton.

MINNA

(Reproachfully)

Klottie, behave!

KLOTTIE

(Looking at ARNIE suspiciously)

How do we know you?

ROBB

Madam Benedicks. I'm here to represent my family. I'm Gundi's stepson.

KLOTTIE

Gundi?

ROBB

Maurice Gundi, the film director. He's in Europe now, working on a film so he asked me to –

KLOTTIE

(To MINNA)

That Gundi! Our Gundi! That dear little toad of a Gundi. Of course he was a witty toad, and a very good lover. I had him in 1931? Yes?

MINNA

According to you, you had everyone in '31.

KLOTTIE

No, it was '30 when I was married to Einfeld.
(To ROBB)
You know of Hector Einfeld, the boulevardier playwright? *The Courtship of Kiki.*

ROBB

I love that play.

KLOTTIE

Do you? A dreadful play. How I betrayed Einfeld. You can always betray a playwright. It gives them plots. But you can't betray an actor. It gives them shingles. I was always faithful to Anton.
(To ARNIE)
Do you know why he insisted I be with him all the time? Tell them, Minna. Say it! Say it!

MINNA

He said… he said you were too ugly to kiss goodbye.

(MINNA breaks out in an irrepressible, mischievous laugh, as KLOTTIE strikes her with her handbag, playfully, amused by the recollection.)

KLOTTIE

What a wit he was! There is nobody left to insult me with such charm. Not my poor Minna. She has no more talent for insults than she had for the stage. Anton's own flesh and blood, but none of his acting genius. Once, in Vienna, some foolish impresario wanted to cast her as Camille because she was so slender, so beautiful, and she could do a heartbreaking cough. Anton advised her to refuse the offer. "You're too young, too healthy, a soubrette, not a leading lady," he warned. That was before she married the aristocratic idiot Von Schott and they settled on his estate at Haldenstein.

MINNA
(Correcting)

Forchtenstein.

KLOTTIE

Suddenly Austria changes from everyday nasty anti-Semitic: the spit, the curse and the broken window, becomes murder and robbery, and the Baron decides that he and his dear young Jewish wife must escape to France before the Gestapo finds her.

MINNA

They don't want to hear this. Nor do I.

KLOTTIE

So he drives to Hungary and hires a pilot in Budapest to fly them to Le Bourget, and of course, the goddamned Nazi pilot betrays them and flies them into Templehoff in Berlin. The Baron is released but she, this… this… this… Minna, is sent to a concentration camp.

MINNA

No more, Klottie! I will not listen to my life whistled through your dentures.

KLOTTIE

You resent my finding comfort in your misfortunes on the very day I need such consolation?
(Undeterred)
Imagine, this one survives her years in the German camp, only to be liberated by the Soviets, and she is foolish enough to admit to them that she is the Baroness von Schott, and they send her to prison in Moscow, then to a gulag in Siberia for being a degenerate aristocrat – and a suspected spy. Is that not the unluckiest life that has ever been lived? Yes? Yes?

ROBB

Yes. Yes.

KLOTTIE

Anton goes to Eleanor Roosevelt at the U.N. and they arrange for her release. She comes to America for her next life, no more Minna the Baroness but Minna the burden.

MINNA

Nonsense. I found work as soon as I regained my strength.

KLOTTIE

Anton would never have taken that horrid small part of the Nazi in the national tour of *Sound of Music* if he didn't have to pay for your stay in that hospital. You know how he was killed? By hearing that "Doe a deer" night after night after night.

MINNA

Stop it, Klottie. That was years before he died.

KLOTTIE

Everything happens to you and you walk away, alive, and still beautiful. And me? What will become of me? Alone and abandoned.

MINNA

You'll always have your complaints for company. No more. Today is about Anton. Not you. Or me.

KLOTTIE

You're right! Anton deserved better from me. Even *I* deserved better than me. God, that I could throw myself deep into his open grave and disappear forever.

> (*She begins to weep, sobbing fiercely, and clings to MINNA, who pats her shoulder, comforting her. The boys look about, uncertain as to what is expected of them. We hear a husky lightly-accented voice offstage commenting on the scene. BRIGITTA, a beautiful, middle-aged woman wearing a veil appears and goes directly to the mourning women.*)

BRIGITTA

What grave? You had him cremated!

KLOTTIE

You're here!!!

BRIGITTA

Where else would I be? Anton was my great friend! Now pull yourself together Klottie. I will help you get through this.

KLOTTIE

You waste your time. I will not survive this.

(BRIGITTA removes a large food parcel from her voluminous handbag.)

BRIGITTA

Here, I made you some of my Chicken Brigitta to get you through the next few days. One dish for Klottie, and one for the skinny Minnie.

(Turning to MINNA)

Well, Minna. Have you thought it over?

MINNA

I have. Meine antwort darauf ist immer noch nein. *["My answer to that is still no."]*

BRIGITTA

If you think anyone else wants it, you're crazy!

MINNA

I don't care who wants it. It's not for sale.

BRIGITTA

Who would treat it better than me? Who? Who?

(Looking at ROBB, interested)

Who's this?

ROBB

Robb Rhinehardt.

BRIGITTA

Not some grandson of my dear Max, are you? I studied with Max in Berlin.

ROBB

I know. When you were Brigitta von Schlegel.

BRIGITTA

You do know a great deal about me, don't you?

ROBB

Of course I do. I'm Maurice Gundi's stepson.

BRIGITTA

Gundi? My Gundi? Well, Klottie, isn't it nice that two young men come to mourn Anton with us? We should have had sons.

(To ROBB and ARNIE)

You two – be her sons today – she needs all the help she can get.

ROBB

Of course. It's easy to be the son of anyone but your own parents.

BRIGITTA

Aren't you clever? You must be a writer?

ROBB

I am! We are.

BRIGITTA
(Pointing to the widow)
Marvelous! Help her through this terrible ordeal.

ROBB

We'll do what we can.

BRIGITTA

Watch her! She's given to fainting. It is low blood pressure mixed with grief and cheap kosher wine.

(KLOTTIE lets out a heart-wrenching sob.)

BRIGITTA

Klottie, be brave. Nobody loved Anton more than I did. How I tried to help him. And time and again I failed.

MINNA
(Like a curse word)
Budapest!

(ARNIE looks at her, puzzled but fascinated.)

BRIGITTA
(To MINNA)
I warned him, "Don't join committees! Don't sign petitions!" But he wanted to fight fascism in red ink with his Waterman pen. Those days you could risk your career just by signing an autograph for the wrong person.
(To ROBB and ARNIE)
Once his name appeared on that blacklist – films – kaput! TV – finis! Poor Anton.

(The RABBI enters.)

RABBI

Mrs. Benedicks, we are going the start the ceremony shortly. Would you please come this way? Madam Brigitta, yes? An honor. I've been a great fan of all your –

MINNA

Indeed. How discerning of you.

(To KLOTTIE)

Come, Klottie. It's time.

BRIGITTA

(To RABBI)

Rabbi? You, yes you my darling fan of a Rabbi, take them inside. But give me a moment more to steady my nerves. I loved him so.

MINNA

Budapest!

(MINNA takes KLOTTIE's arm and enters the chapel with the RABBI.)

BRIGITTA

(To ROBB and ARNIE)

You two – stay with me! I don't want to upstage the mourners with my grief.

(ROBB, ARNIE and BRIGITTA are now alone in the ante room of the chapel.)

BRIGITTA

I'm desperate. These women could drive one mad. Hopeless and helpless. What a pair.

ROBB

Anything we can do?

BRIGITTA

Take care of them today. It's a great deal to ask but they have no one now. I'll take care of the widow Klottie but it's the other one, that Minna who needs looking after. She's crazy, you know?

ROBB

No?

BRIGITTA

But she won't let me help her. I have Morton D. Segal of Kensington Films in London ready to finance the movie. I have De Sica in Rome telling me he would love to direct it with the right script. And still she says no.

ARNIE

I don't understand. What film is this?

BRIGITTA

Why, *The Minna Benedicks Story*.

ROBB

Great, great idea! Gorgeous woman faces the monstrous forces of fascism and communism in one amazing lifetime and survives.

BRIGITTA

Wrong! When Brigitta plays her she does not survive – she prevails.

ARNIE

You're planning to play her yourself?

BRIGITTA
(*Sarcastically, as if to a very dumb child*)

No. I want to play Eleanor Roosevelt!

ROBB
(*Enthusiastically*)

You'd be great in either role.

BRIGITTA

I may be a few years older than Minna was when all that happened to her, but trust me, I'll be a better Minna than Minna ever was.

ROBB

I'm sure that's true.

BRIGITTA

But nothing I say can convince her. Money won't do it. Nor will the promise of fame and immortality.

ROBB
(*Looking at ARNIE, pointedly*)

Some people don't know their own best interests.

BRIGITTA

Well, I hope you do.

ROBB

What do you want us to do?

BRIGITTA

Convince Minna to sell me the rights to her life story.

ARNIE

But we just met her. If you can't do it, how can we?

BRIGITTA

(To ROBB)

A good-looking young lover would make her see her life *differently.*

ARNIE

You want him to get you the rights by... by...? He can't do that!

BRIGITTA

Why not?

ARNIE

That's exploitation. No one has a right to hurt that woman after what she's endured.

ROBB

(Defending the idea)

Hurt? Who says she's going to be hurt! Brigitta wants to save her from herself.

BRIGITTA

Yes, that's the gist of it. She's still a beautiful woman. Oh, don't I know what it is for an older woman to need a young man? And vice versa.

(She lifts her veil, stares at one, then the other.)

I've already written the treatment myself. All you have to do is fill in the dialogue.

ROBB

You mean you'd trust us with a screenplay?

BRIGITTA

Why not? It's only words. I am not some ruthless movie star trying to exploit some poor woman. I will give Minna a life she never had. She was a victim. Once I play her on screen, she can hold up her head again. A world-renowned figure. As she deserves to be.

ROBB

You'll bring her back from the dead!

BRIGITTA

Think of what's best for Minna. And while you're at it, think of what's good for you.

(She drops her cigarette to floor and vigorously stamps it out.)

Now, I must join them. They need someone to direct their grief other than that star struck Rabbi.

(She exits through door into chapel.)

ARNIE

Come on, let's get out of here. This is meshuggah.

ROBB

Crazy? What's so crazy is you wanting to walk out now.

ARNIE

Robb, do you know what she's asking you to do?

ROBB

Brigitta was just being European. Make nice to Minna. That's all Brigitta was saying.

ARNIE

That's not what I heard.

ROBB

Okay, so Minna needs a little romancing.

ARNIE

You mean fucking!

ROBB

Same thing in Hungarian.

ARNIE

Brigitta smells our desperation and she wants one of us to seduce that poor woman into giving permission to have her life filmed. Well, that's not going to be me.

ROBB

You're saying I have to do it?

ARNIE

Try your damndest, but I don't see you getting that woman to sell her life story.

ROBB

But you could.

ARNIE

What?

ROBB

You've got to do it!

ARNIE

Why?

ROBB

Look, with any luck I'll be able to get Gundi to help me. He'll push my work. But you –

ARNIE

What work is that? The scripts I've written? And you polished?

ROBB

If we don't get our careers moving, I got to go it alone as a producer. Sure, once I make it I'll try to help you. Did I say that? Do you believe that? I can't believe this shit is I, but this shit is me!

ARNIE

No, this is what you'd like to be. Not what you are. I saw you last summer in Mississippi on the freedom march. You're the guy who gave the finger to that Sheriff and nearly –

ROBB

Shmuck, it's easier to face a bigot than to face your own failure. Arnie, we are offered a once in a lifetime chance! Walk away and its grad school for you. A lifetime teaching "Shakespeare to O'Neill" to kids with small talent and big dreams.

ARNIE

You mean guys like me?

ROBB

No. You're a terrific writer. Trouble is – talent alone can't cut it these days. You need the right contacts. And Brigitta is nothing *but* contacts.

ARNIE

Okay, *you* think this is such a great idea? You go in there and comfort Minna.

ROBB

I can't.

ARNIE

Of course you can't! In your heart of hearts you know it's wrong.

ROBB

(*Annoyed*)

Stop imposing your fucking virtues on me. I am what you see. Nothing more. Nothing less. I think she's fantastic. I love older women. And this one is special. She's a prime piece – of history.

ARNIE

Then don't let me stop you from making history.

ROBB

You couldn't – if I could.

ARNIE

What are you talking about?

ROBB

Well...this little engine...can't.

ARNIE

What?

ROBB

It sort of stopped working last February.

ARNIE

You over wound it. Clockwise, always clockwise.

ROBB

I'm not kidding.

ARNIE

Please! Why every other night I come back from work and I see that you put the white towel on the outside doorknob. Why, I've walked around the village for hours trying to give you privacy with some girl.

ROBB

Those towels were... were... wishful fucking!

ARNIE

You didn't have to lie to me!

ROBB

If it never happened to you, you don't know how terrible it is. It's so bad I went to see a shrink with that birthday check that Gundi sent me. The good doctor said it's not hopeless; that I just gotta learn to relax.

ARNIE

Look, your doctor is right. You'll get better. It takes time.

ROBB

But we don't have time. Arnie, we lose this chance and it could be years before we catch some luck.

(Bitterly, tearfully)

I'm a prisoner in my own fucking skin, and I can't break out.

(Seriously)

Until we met Brigitta today I was seriously thinking about... Hell, I only came here to see what it was like to be dead. Being ashes in that urn is not half as bad as being me – alive. But when Brigitta spoke, I saw a future for me... for us.

ARNIE

Look, I – I will talk to the woman. I don't know what I'm gonna say, but I'll talk to her. Nothing more!

ROBB

That's all I ask. She says no, and we're no worse off than we are now.

ARNIE

No. I can't. I won't embarrass that woman or myself.

ROBB

So? Go home, forget the whole goddamned business. But tell me? Why did you come here today, if not to open a door?

LIGHTS OUT

ACT ONE

Scene Two

(Minna's walkup apartment on the Upper West Side. A collection of thrift shop furniture, arranged with taste, a blanket covering the tears in a sofa in the living room, some photographs on the wall, a Pullman kitchen is in the room. A small corridor leads to an unseen bedroom. MINNA enters, followed by ARNIE, tosses her mourning hat on sofa, and loosens her hair. She is strikingly attractive as she turns and gestures towards him to sit on the bed-sofa.)

MINNA

Setzen zie sich bitte! Sit! Sit. Sit. Coffee? Black? White?

ARNIE

I don't want to put you to any —

MINNA

You don't. It's already made. I keep it in that thermos over there. Just pour.

(ARNIE pours two cups of coffee from the thermos and holds up the cream.)

No milk for me. There's some shnecken in the breadbox. It's not so fresh but it's still edible. Take a piece, it's okay.

(ARNIE reaches into breadbox and starts chewing on a piece of schnecken.)

ARNIE

Thanks. Were you very close to your brother?

MINNA

When I was a child, yes. But he was so much older than I was. Anton treated me more like his daughter than his sister. And you heard Klottie. I wouldn't be alive today if not for him.

ARNIE

You do have a great story to tell.

MINNA

Not all great stories have to be told. Or sold.

ARNIE

But you shouldn't let people forget what happened.

MINNA

Some things are best left where they are.

ARNIE

Collecting dust?

MINNA

It's the dust that holds them together. Fragile things so easily fall apart when examined.

ARNIE

There's no way you're going to sell your story to Brigitta?

MINNA

Don't tell me! Is that why you're here? She asked you to?

ARNIE
(A beat, then softly)

Yes! That's why I'm here. She asked us to.

MINNA

How refreshing! The boy tells the truth. I like that.

ARNIE

Why won't you sell it? You must need the money

MINNA

I get by. I work as a clerk in a pharmacy on Broadway and Seventy-Sixth Street. I am the counter cosmetician. I peddle lipsticks and cosmetics. I'm quite good at it. With one twist of my tongue, I can turn some greasy goop to glamorous gloss and change wrinkles into laugh lines. I can sell everything. People believe me. It's a gift. But I will not sell the only part of myself that still belongs to me. What do you see?

(She thrusts a photograph of herself when young into his hands.)

ARNIE

A beautiful woman. You haven't changed all that much.

MINNA

Budapest!

ARNIE

What?

MINNA

My term for bullshit. When I lived in Europe, Budapest was the world capitol of lies and flattery, of charming deceits, and cruel betrayals.

ARNIE

But you are. Beautiful. You must know that you are.

MINNA

(She indicates her face, slapping her own cheek lightly.)
This face? No.
(She taps her photograph.)
That photograph? Yes. When I see poor Brigitta, I know how awful it must be to try to keep up the illusion. The surgically pulled flesh, the artful scars hiding behind the ears, covered by the rebellious blond wig. Aach, such glamour! Cracked porcelain with all the repairs showing. You see, she cannot play me. I can't allow that. I was young when life happened to me. Just twenty-two. Even when she was young, she was old.

ARNIE

She seemed to admire Anton so much.

MINNA

Please. So she made hot soup for him when he had his bouts with bronchitis? She even got down on her hands and knees and scrubbed the kitchen floor, because Klottie is such a sow. But did she pick up a phone and call her friends in Hollywood to get him a job? Never! What does she know of suffering or sacrifice? Or friendship?

ARNIE

But he was blacklisted, right? She couldn't have –

MINNA

More like a grey-list. He was getting on in years. Even if there were no blacklist she wouldn't have helped him.

ARNIE

Is that why you won't sell your story to her? Because she didn't help him in Hollywood?

MINNA

No. If she had gotten my brother a starring role in a movie, or a decent part in a Broadway play, I still would not have done it. Some things cannot be bought with the promise of a fame I don't want, I can't use, and I won't have.

(A beat, as she looks at him)

Or with handsome, ambitious young boys.

ARNIE

You didn't think that I would –

MINNA

No? How disappointing.

ARNIE

You mean you'd like it if I did?

MINNA

Am I so disagreeable? Distasteful? Displeasing?

ARNIE

No. Not at all.

MINNA

Good. I will take you at your word. The young man does not find me unpleasant, distasteful or displeasing.

ARNIE

Don't. Please. You're embarrassing both of us.

MINNA

You can only stop me with more truth.

ARNIE

She did ask us. She said we could write the screenplay if you… Oh, hell. I should be going. Forgive me. I'm so sorry. I feel like such a prick.

MINNA

Why? I'm not offended or surprised. And I can use your company. So, tell me about yourself. What is an Artie Forman?

ARNIE

Arnie. But you can call me whatever you want. Start with "cunning little bastard," if you want.

MINNA

What *do* you want, my cunning little bastard?

ARNIE

You couldn't care about that. Not on the day you buried your brother.

MINNA

What better way to deal with grief? Nothing is more interesting than a young man starting out in life. A young man with kind dark eyes, trembling hands and a code of honor. How long have you wanted to be a screenwriter?

(She takes his hand in her own, stares at him with interest, determined to seduce him.)

ARNIE

Always.

MINNA

But why movies?

ARNIE

I don't dream. Oh I suppose I do, but I can't remember them. Never have.

MINNA

Really? How awful.

ARNIE

You see, I close my eyes, and fall sleep, then I wake up, and between the sleep and the awakening – nothing. But when I write screenplays in my mind, they feel like dreams, or at least, what other people tell me dreams must be.

MINNA

(Joking)

And they say I had a hard life? Poor boy. Without dreams I could never have survived my years in the camps. At first I did what any well brought up young Jewish girl would do. I blamed myself for my predicament.

ARNIE

How could you?

MINNA

Easily. I told myself that I was not a good daughter. I often put off seeing my parents with some ridiculous excuse. They were so dear, but so boring. Once, in Vienna – a few years before the Anschluss – I was rushing off to the opera. On my way there I saw my father walking alone down near the Ringstrasse, looking old and disconsolate. And I failed to stop my taxicab to say hello. I didn't want his rough-bearded kiss against my cheek to spoil my makeup. I didn't want to look into his troubled eyes. Later I told myself if I had stopped and said hello and kissed him, God would have spared me all that was to follow in the years to come. Worse, I had married the Baron against their wishes. And in a Cathedral. It was not because he was a Catholic that they objected, but because they knew I did not love him. So, I had been a bad daughter, a faithless Jew, a foolish wife, a woman who had married for ease and pleasure. God saw my wickedness and punished me for my sins by preventing my escape from Europe.

ARNIE

You didn't really believe that.

MINNA

No. Not for long. Soon, even I knew that God had nothing to do with that camp. I was there, not by design, but through an accident of birth. So I taught myself to shut away the odors, the cruelty and the despair, and dream of my world before the war. All in soft black and white, a gelatin silver print of my young life. In that dream I was a great artist who could bring comfort to the world, and, of course, glory to myself! I had such a beautiful singing voice. Just listen to this!

(*She goes to an old-fashioned phonograph and plays a recording of a soprano singing a Viennese waltz. The song plays through to the end of the scene.*)

ARNIE

Is that you singing?

MINNA

In my dreams.

ARNIE

What do you mean?

MINNA

I found it by chance a few months ago in a twenty-five cents bin in front of a junk shop on Columbus Avenue. The wonderful thing was that I had this very recording when I was a child. I would play it and move my lips to it, and pretend that I was the soprano, Josephine Fisher-Haupt. Do you know of her?

ARNIE

No.

MINNA

She had a great career in Salzburg before the war. They say she collaborated, but that's nonsense. She was Austrian and the Austrians were the Nazis. In the camp, I could recall her voice, and I found a way to insert it in my dreams. Background music to my delusions. In those dreams my sweet mother and father, who died in Auschwitz, were still alive reading all the morning newspapers over little cups of Turkish coffee.

ARNIE

Why didn't you leave while there was still time?

MINNA

You live in a world of museums and opera, of Fisher-Haupt, fine furs and French tulips, and excellent Turkish coffee... you convince yourself that the goosestep is a temporary fad. The Devil's tango. Mozart will not allow this to happen. Mozart will rise from his grave and stop it with a Sonatina. But Mozart slept, and it happened.

ARNIE

I'm sorry.

MINNA

(She turns away, not wanting him to see her emotion)

This is new. This is something altogether new. I could not have survived if I was this weepy then. Now pee, wash your hands, and come to bed!

ARNIE

You serious?

MINNA

No. I want to stay here all night weeping and watch you eat stale schnecken.

(Suddenly serious, softer, almost pleading)

Anton not only saved me from the Soviets, he saved me from America. He would sit there, right where you are, and spin out tales of my childhood, and tell me stories of my sweet parents that I had never known, or had half forgotten. When Anton died, he was the last to remember them, or me before. What a beautiful word – "before." And he took that with him to the grave. So I am trapped in the goddamned Technicolor present, with you, my young friend. And I need you to help me escape from me for a little while. Are you frightened?

ARNIE

No! No.

MINNA

Budapest!

ARNIE

A little.

MINNA

It's all right. So am I.

(She reaches out to him. He takes her hand, studies it for a moment, then kisses it. The voice of the singer soars as the)

LIGHTS FADE OUT

ACT ONE

Scene Three

(Six months later. The same apartment, except for a portable typewriter set up on the kitchen table, and an untidy pile of papers beside it by the phone. ARNIE sits typing as MINNA enters, having come home from work. She looks at him, shakes her head, smiles.)

MINNA

Nothing?

ARNIE

Her secretary said she'd call me after five. She had some news. Well, it's half-past five and still no call.

MINNA

She'll call. People get tied up.

ARNIE

Like me. I'm a giant knot from toes to ears. There's a little bit of hair up here, to the left of my part, that's relaxed but then that's because there are no nerves in hair follicles.

(The TELEPHONE rings. He stares at it, waits a moment, then rushes to answer it.)

ARNIE

Yes, Sally. Yes. Did they say anything else? They liked the dialogue – okay. And the story was ingenious. Thanks. Oh. Yes. Keep trying.

(He hangs up phone, turns to MINNA.)

Universal has something like it in development. It was too grim for MGM. And Paramount isn't buying westerns these days. And the story department at Columbia hasn't gotten around to reading it. But the others all liked the writing so she'll keep sending it out... to television. A sample script – for *Gunsmoke*.

MINNA

But they liked it? Yes?

ARNIE

Doesn't matter. They passed. Trust me, *Gunsmoke* is going to pass too.

MINNA

It was a fine script.

ARNIE

Maybe. But it didn't sell. I wasted my time. And your money.

MINNA

What money? I haven't given you any money.

ARNIE

Minna, I am living off you.

MINNA

Nonsense. You do more than your share.

ARNIE

My share? You pay the rent, buy the food, and pay for the illusion that I have some talent.

MINNA

It was too good for them.

ARNIE

Don't! It's what every failure uses as an excuse.

MINNA

Why are you so hard on yourself?

ARNIE

Wrong question. Why are you so easy on me?

MINNA

Because I honor talent. I read your screenplay and it thrilled me.

ARNIE

Budapest.

MINNA

All right. It amused me. I loved westerns as a child. I adored Tom Mix. Every Saturday my governess would take me to this little theatre off the Josefstadt and we would watch one of his cowboy films. Oh, how I wanted to grow up to be one of those tough talking girls in the honky-tonk saloon who lifts a ruffled skirt, shows the fancy garter on her thigh, growls out a song, and dies for the hero she loves.

ARNIE

You're a wonderful woman. How did I get so lucky?

MINNA

Come, let's go to bed.

ARNIE

Goddamn it, is that your cure for everything?

MINNA

My mother used mustard plasters and camphorated oil. I think my way is preferable.

ARNIE

You can't tease me out of this one. I am seriously depressed. Speaking of mothers, mine called to remind me that the Jewish holidays were coming up and she'd like me to be there. She assured me that she wouldn't live forever –

MINNA

Like someone she wouldn't dare mention. You should go.

ARNIE

No. Look, if she can learn to accept my sister's Italian boyfriend, she can damn well accept you.

MINNA

He's Italian. I'm old. A mother prefers that her children go for the pasta rather than the palsy.

ARNIE

You're not old.

MINNA

No. As my mother would say, "I'm in my second youth."

ARNIE

She thinks you're feeding me dope to keep me here. She warned me that you work in a drugstore, so you had easy access to opiates.

MINNA

God, that I did! I'd pop a few now. Or is it "drop a few?"

ARNIE

What's wrong?

MINNA

I had the most... the most peculiar day. Business was slow, the rain didn't help, but in the morning, around eleven, this strange man comes into the pharmacy. I noticed him because he was dressed as if he was going to an elegant afternoon party. In 1932. You know, a belted camel's hair coat, a stiff shirt collar and a neat black tie, freshly barbered, a fedora tilted rakishly on the head, and grey pigskin gloves. Who wears gloves in May? And he carried a really fine English umbrella. It had a dog's head carved in bone on the handle.

ARNIE

A dandy.

MINNA

Trust me, you don't see many in my pharmacy. Junkies, yes? Dandies, no! He comes to my counter and says he wants to buy some toiletries from me, asking me which I prefer, and of course, I point to our most expensive scent. It's what we call in the smell trade, *un parfum tres cher*. I sold him that in the largest size we carry, some matching bath oils and powder, and the poor innocent just kept nodding and buying.

ARNIE

I didn't know you could be so ruthless.

MINNA

You should see me at work. I am merciless Minna. And when I have the rare, rich customer, my avarice is unbridled. This man, he just keeps staring at me. Then he asks me if I gift-wrap. "Oui, Monsieur!" I gift-wrap. I hand a glorious be-ribboned package back to him, and he says, "It's for you, Madame. Pour vous." Then, before I can even protest, he bows, and leaves the shop.

ARNIE

You have an admirer! I'm jealous. Did he give you those flowers too?

MINNA

Certainly not! They come from my favorite florist – the Korean grocer.

ARNIE

Was that all?

MINNA

Well, he kept coming back. I'd say he would arrive at the store every two hours, just to look at me.

ARNIE

No more gifts?

MINNA

Just a lot of stares. And shy, stealthy, embarrassed smiles.

ARNIE

With the pigskin glove still on?

MINNA

No. He removed one glove, and displayed the most amazing star sapphire ring on his finger. So I walked over to him to return the gift to his hand. And he said "Keep it, ma cher Madam. Please, it would break my heart." So I kept it. I didn't want to be responsible for any more heartbreak. And I can use the perfume.

(The DOORBELL rings.)

ARNIE

You expecting someone?

MINNA

No. It must be Klottie. Who else arrives without calling first? She's been feeling very low lately, so she wanted to come by and be reassured that nothing good had happened to *me*.

(ARNIE answers the door. KLOTTIE looks him over disapprovingly, and enters. She says nothing, goes to MINNA, kisses her on both cheeks.)

KLOTTIE

You're not looking well. Not at all well. All that work, work, work.
(She looks disdainfully at ARNIE and hands him her coat.)
Well, I suppose someone has to work or you'd both starve.
(She picks up a page of his manuscript.)
You write on a machine? I remember my lover, the great Franz Werfel, saying that a typewriter was for secretaries, that he couldn't create by placing his fingers on the noisy keys of a –

MINNA

But *he* can!

KLOTTIE

He's no writer!

MINNA

How can you say that? You've never read his work.

KLOTTIE

I don't need to. Look how you live. Every great writer I've ever known loves luxury.

ARNIE

What about Gorki?

KLOTTIE

Especially Gorki. I remember him telling me that the best way to write about "The Lower Depths" is from a suite at the Ritz.

ARNIE

You made that up?

KLOTTIE
(Ignoring him)
Possibly. I'm not here to squander my fascinating past in banter with you, boy. I want to speak with Minna.

MINNA

Speak.

KLOTTIE

Privately.

(ARNIE rises, but MINNA gestures for him to take his seat again.)

MINNA

I keep no secrets from Arnold.

KLOTTIE

Thank God for that.

MINNA

Why?

KLOTTIE

If you keep no secrets from him, you can't still love him. I'm broke.

MINNA

I got paid yesterday. If you need twenty to tide you over –

KLOTTIE

Never! How could I borrow from you? You are just a step away from the streets yourself. The day will come when those lovely fingers will be crippled with arthritis, when you won't be able to sell your cosmetics from the counter, when this whole façade, this Potemkin's village of a face of yours will surrender to the wrinkles and the chicken feet –

MINNA

Crow's feet.

KLOTTIE

Crows. Chickens. *Tout le même poulet*. How will you live? When you can't support him, will he be here for you? No!

MINNA

Klottie, what business is this of yours?

KLOTTIE

You should be ashamed of that question! I'm your last living relative. We only have each other. I stay up nights worrying about you. I can't help you later… but I can help you now.

MINNA

Say another word and you leave.

KLOTTIE

Tochtin.

ARNIE

What's a Tochtin?

KLOTTIE

Unlike you, wretched boy, a Tochtin is rich. Early sixties, long widowed, lonely, romantic, childless, and looking for a wife.

MINNA

You've found your mouse? Pounce!

KLOTTIE

Tochtin and me? Nonsense. This is America. It is beauty, beauty, beauty they want here. All I have is a little pep, some zip, and plenty of gusto. He looks to me for a friend, not for a future wife. He collects rare books. Mostly about theatre. How did we meet? I'm glad you asked. I put a classified ad in *The Times*.

MINNA

You advertised for a *friend?* I didn't think *The Times* took personal ads.

KLOTTIE

No. I was under antiques and collectibles.

ARNIE

Is that how you see yourself?

KLOTTIE

Shush! I had all these old Viennese theatre programs to sell, and some wonderful posters and show cards of Anton, and when Tochtin, the buyer, found out I was Anton's widow, he was beside himself with pleasure. A great fan of Anton's. A man of culture. Dignity. But a man without a family. Lost everyone in the camps. He came to this country in '47, a penniless survivor, worked hard and built an air conditioning factory. Soon another factory, and another, and another. Made his fortune on cold air. What could be more modern?

MINNA

Enough with this Tochtin! I even hate his name.

KLOTTIE

(Ignoring her)

Lives in style. A duplex off Fifth Avenue. No view of the park, but you can see the trees if you stick your head out the bathroom window and look to the west. Who needs a view? Not me. Not you. We've had our views. You should see him when he enters a room. That camel's hair coat, the jaunty fedora hat, the starched shirt collar, the dark tie, the yellow pigskin gloves, and that gorgeous star sapphire ring blazing away on his manicured hands. Not to mention that darling little old world moustache. You should see him when he –

MINNA

I have! Today.

ARNIE

So that was Tochtin?

KLOTTIE

Well, I couldn't invite him to my apartment to meet you, could I? So I let him know where you worked so he could see you for himself. He saw, he liked. No, *he admired.* He wants to meet you. Trust me, he's yours for the taking. And it's not as if you never married for money. You would never have eloped with that idiot Egon if he weren't –

MINNA

Klottie, the choice is yours. I can grab your shoulders and throw you down the stairs. Or you can leave on your own and walk away with all your limbs working. But leave.

KLOTTIE

If you don't marry this man, I'll end up on the streets. I know it.

MINNA

No. You've put away just enough to keep you in the lap of misery for years to come.

KLOTTIE

So, keep the boy if you must, and marry Tochtin. *That one* can live here... say he's your nephew... and you, you're living in style off Fifth Avenue.

MINNA

Without a view of the park? Never!

KLOTTIE

At least meet the man.

MINNA

I have. Once was quite enough.

KLOTTIE

You never knew your own best interests. Do you think I want to meddle in your life? Who am I to meddle in anyone's life? What was mine? A diorama of disappointment, disaster and despair. But Anton begged me to take care of his little sister when he was gone. So I am taking care in the only way I know. Forget your selfish pleasure with this boy. He's ruining whatever chance you have left, and you're shielding him from the hard realities of the world. But I don't give a damn about him. I don't want to help him. Ruin him if that pleases you! I wouldn't lift a finger to save him.

ARNIE

Thank you, Jesus.

KLOTTIE

You exhaust me with your stubbornness, Minna. But I have a duty to honor my pledge to Anton. Listen carefully. This is no country to grow old in. It has no memory, no past, only contempt for yesterday. And we are yesterday. If you don't seize this chance, I will give up on you forever.

MINNA

Fine. You've done your best for me. I'm not worth the effort. How much did you expect to get from your Tochtin for arranging the match?

KLOTTIE

What has this boy done to you? He's stolen your faith in humanity. The most precious thing we have. He's using you, Minna. Using you.

MINNA
To ARNIE)

She thinks you're using me. Are you using me?
(ARNIE nods.)

Yes, he says he is. I certainly hope he is. It's so, so flattering to think that after all these years I can still be used by someone – who's young and charming.

KLOTTIE
(Shocked)

God in heaven, you are in love with him. This is worse than I imagined.

(There is a loud BUZZ. MINNA goes to the intercom.)

MINNA

Yes. Who is it?

ROBB'S VOICE

Minna, its Robb. Is Arnie there?

MINNA
(To ARNIE)

You want to see him?
(ARNIE shrugs his assent.)
(To intercom)

I'm buzzing you in. Yes, he's here.
(To ARNIE)

Did you two quarrel?

ARNIE

We always quarrel. What else are friends for?

MINNA

Do you want me to go into the bedroom with Klottie and leave you two alone to talk?

ARNIE

No. Stay. I'm in no mood for his bullshit.

(DOORBELL rings. ROBB enters.)

ROBB

Hello everyone.
(No one answers him.)
Who died?

ARNIE

I did. The studios passed on *The Widowmaker*. My agent's going to try TV but even that's a long shot.

ROBB

Well, I thought it was a terrific script. I knew those shit-heads wouldn't appreciate it.

ARNIE

Don't you tell me I'm too good to be a success?

ROBB

No. You're just too good to be a failure. I sent the script to Gundi to read. He loved it. He thought that De Sica might want to make a spaghetti western, so he sent it on to Vittorio. And... and... De Sica loved it too.

ARNIE
(Excited)
De Sica wants to make it?

ROBB

Well, not quite. He admired your writing. He said he wants to work with you – should the right project come along.

ARNIE

Did he happen to mention what that right project might be?

ROBB

Yes, he told me. But I promised Brigitta I'd let her tell you herself.

ARNIE

It isn't what I think it is?

ROBB

Look, I'm not allowed to speak about it until she's here. I thought she'd be here now. She was supposed to be here before me. Remember "Diamond Dolly" when she always arrived late and how it pissed off Gary Cooper.

ARNIE

Not Cooper. It was Randolph Scott.

ROBB

Definitely Cooper.

(*The downstairs INTERCOM buzzes persistently.*)

That's her. Remember how the deaf-mute servant, Sam Jaffe, hit a gong whenever she appeared in *White Goddess*?

ARNIE

Herbert Marshall and Jimmy Stewart? Right?

ROBB

Wrong. Robert Donat and George Brent.

ARNIE

You sure about Robert Donat?

ROBB

Positive. Brigitta screened it for me last week.

(*The DOORBELL rings and MINNA answers it. She is confronted by a BRIGITTA with a handful of Chinese take-out menus, which she uses to fan herself.*)

BRIGITTA

Why do all these Chinese restaurants paper your hallway with their menus? You could get a headache from the MSG just from touching them. He's told you about De Sica?

ROBB

Yes.

ARNIE

It doesn't amount to much, does it?

BRIGITTA

It means a great deal. He's a great artist. Great artists need great subjects.

(She stares at MINNA)

Vittorio told me once that he wasted too much of his life during the war years in Italy. To survive he made all those silly romantic films where the heroine was always talking into a white telephone to her lover, and nobody ever referred to the fascism that had taken over Italy. He wants to make up for all that in his new films. And he has. He wants grit. Purpose. Reality. Significance. Life. And death. After *The Bicycle Thief* he's been searching for another subject that will satisfy that need.

ARNIE

A film about starving sewer workers drowning in shit during the Depression?

BRIGITTA

Don't be facetious. You know what he wants. It's what we all want.

(She turns and looks at MINNA.)

ARNIE

But it's not what she wants.

BRIGITTA

Minna, I won't beg you. I don't beg. But the utter selfishness of your refusal appalls me.

ARNIE

Selfish? For trying to protect her privacy?

BRIGITTA

If Anna Frank had survived the camps do you think that she would have destroyed her Diary and refused to have it filmed to protect her privacy? Never. It's a mere nineteen years since the war ended, and already the Holocaust deniers are saying it never happened.

(She takes out a newspaper and slaps it on the table.)

Look at this article by some awful Frenchman. "The Holocaust - A Modern Myth." He claims that the only reason for the German gas chambers and the ovens was to destroy the bodies of the sick workers who had died of typhus. It wasn't genocide, it was just good hygiene.

BRIGITTA (Continued)

And if that isn't bad enough, see how the world ignores the gulags. The Soviets are keeping so many innocent souls in prison there – even the great Wallenberg – savior of a thousand Hungarian Jews – may be alive, wasting away in some Siberian camp. And for you not to let the world know how it was for you – how it is for them – that is so selfish – so unworthy of you. If De Sica wants to film your life, you should be honored. Grateful that a great artist will make a marvelous film that could change the world.

ARNIE

You never give up, do you?

BRIGITTA

That was my motto as a young actress. Never give up – but always give in. Come Robbie, I see we're wasting our time here.

MINNA

Stay. I'll order in some Chinese. We've already got the menus.

BRIGITTA

What?

MINNA

One mustn't be a snob about a menu, Brigitta. Chinese food goes well with champagne, even my cheap champagne.

ROBB

What's going on?

MINNA

I want to celebrate.

ARNIE

Celebrate? What? Somebody's birthday?

KLOTTIE

(Delighted)

Tochtin! She is going to marry my Tochtin! I knew it. You've come to your senses at last.

BRIGITTA

Who is this Tochtin?

MINNA

Some rich friend of Klottie's. She's playing matchmaker.

KLOTTIE

He is offering her a life of comfort and luxury.

MINNA

And I am refusing it, as you knew I would. Klottie, you waste your schemes on me. I celebrate because... because...
(A long beat)
...I have decided to sell my story to you. Brigitta, you have persuaded me at last. You and the marvelous De Sica.

ARNIE

But you always said –

MINNA

That was before. She's right. The world is forgetting. And I can't. If I can remind them – even in a small way – something good may come out of all that horror.

BRIGITTA

Vittorio will be so happy.

MINNA

He should be. He is not only getting my story to film, he's getting a fine screenwriter to write the screenplay.

ROBB

We'll do a great job with it.

MINNA

Who is this we?! You won't touch it. I mean for Arnie to write the screenplay alone.

ARNIE

Are you sure?

MINNA

As sure as I am of anything.

BRIGITTA

Wonderful! I know Vittorio will agree. He dearly loved that western screenplay he read. Liebchen. I promise you. I will protect your story with my life.
(ROBB opens the champagne and pours out four glasses.)
To *The Minna Benedicks Story*! And to Minna – a great woman, and a wonderful friend.

MINNA
(Laughing)

Budapest.

BRIGITTA

How did you know?

MINNA

Know? What?

BRIGITTA

That's where De Sica wants to film it. In Budapest!

ALL
(Raising their cups)

To Minna. A great woman!

BRIGITTA

And a marvelous movie.

LIGHTS OUT

Scene One

(Three months later. Minna's apartment. The doorbell rings. MINNA goes to open it. ROBB stands there looking distraught.)

MINNA

You want some coffee?

ROBB

No thanks. But I wouldn't refuse a beer.

MINNA

I don't think we have any.

ARNIE

We do. I got some today. But I didn't put it in the fridge. Can you drink it warm?

ROBB

I prefer it warm. It's my latest affectation.

ARNIE

So?

ROBB

No.

ARNIE

You heard from De Sica?

ROBB

Yes.

ARNIE

And?

ROBB

He passed.

ARNIE

When?

ROBB

Friday.

ARNIE

Last Friday? You waited nearly one fucking week to tell me that De Sica passed? While I've been sitting here waiting for –

ROBB

You! You! You! What about me? Your co-producer? I was crushed. And you should have seen Brigitta. Wept, just like some starlet who was turned down for a bit part. She feels he should have gone ahead with the picture even though he thought it was a piece of shit –

ARNIE

What? You are saying De Sica thought it was –

ROBB

Those weren't his exact words. In Italian it sounds more like a curse. "Io Vole Male."

MINNA

I know Italian.

ROBB

Do you know everything?

MINNA
(To ROBB with sadness)

Yes. Unfortunately, I do.

ROBB
(Suddenly excited, laughing out the good news)

Well, you don't know *this*. Gundi's read the script. He loved it. And he's offered to direct it himself. True, he's no De Sica. But Gundi's good – a real craftsman. He was the second unit director on two of David Lean's films. And he directed a few decent German flicks before the war. He knows how to make a picture move.

(ARNIE looks to MINNA for a response.)

MINNA

He's not bad. A few of those films were quite engaging.

ARNIE
(Hopeful, excitedly)

Great. Great! Let us all bow down and worship the Great God Gundi. Minna, you prepare the sacramental wine while I offer flower-bedecked virgins to him. Where the hell do you find a flower bedecked virgin on West 84th Street? When do we meet with him. Is he coming here?

ROBB

No. He works out of his Paris office. Everything is done there.

ARNIE

Paris? Christ, I don't have a passport, how do you get an emergency passport? And the airfare? Is he going to pay the airfare? I don't –

MINNA

Not to worry. I do. A small loan.

ARNIE

I couldn't –

MINNA

You must. He needs you, and I want you working on it. Gundi is no writer, and this one…
                    (*Gesturing towards ROBB*)
…is no… whatever he thinks he is.

ROBB

Thank you, Minna. The great news is that Gundi says he has a shooting script in Arnie's first draft. "Best fooking screenplay I've read in years!" And he wants to cut costs by moving quickly. If he can start filming exteriors this month, the Hungarian government will co-produce it with him and Morton D. Siegel.

MINNA

And Brigitta? She's willing to work with Gundi?

ROBB

Thrilled. He was the cameraman who worked on her first American pictures. He knows her best angles. "He will paint me with light!" – that's what she says. And she's even postponed her salary to get it made. She's gone for a profit-sharing deal. Now if that's not an act of faith, nothing is. Everyone knows how important this picture will be.

MINNA

What of the Soviets? Would they allow the gulag scenes to be filmed in Hungary?

ROBB

Gundi's taken care of that. All the German scenes are going to be shot in Budapest. And all the Russian ones he's going to shoot in West Germany. Of course he doesn't show the whole script to the Hungarians. It takes a Hungarian to trick a Hungarian.

MINNA

So it's finally going to happen.

ARNIE

(Embracing her)

You sound scared?

MINNA

No. Surprised. Nothing ever happens as we plan it, does it? Still, something has happened! And it could be wonderful.

ROBB

Could be? Will be?

MINNA

My God, this is terrible.

ARNIE

What's wrong?

MINNA

Klottie. It's such good news – it could kill her. However shall I break it to her?

(ARNIE embraces MINNA and ROBB joins them in a three-way hug.)

LIGHTS OUT

ACT TWO

Scene Two

(Minna's apartment, a year later, about eight o'clock at night. It is raining outside. They are both dressed for an occasion, ARNIE in a suit and tie, MINNA in her best dress. ARNIE turns to face MINNA.)

ARNIE

Do you like this tie? Be truthful, I got another one if you think this one is too –

MINNA

It's not too – and the color becomes you. Deepens the blue of your eyes.

ARNIE

I don't have blue eyes.

MINNA

(Jesting)

Exactly! A magic necktie. So wear it. You look very handsome tonight. I guess it's time we got started. We have plenty of time. The invitation is for eight. And you should eat something before. Now, you have a choice. I've got some Bavarian ham, some pepper brie, and some nice brown bread. Or we can have the roast chicken. I can whip up some potatoes and –

ARNIE

Nothing for me.

MINNA

They won't be serving anything till after the screening.

ARNIE

I couldn't eat now. Or ever again.

MINNA

Darling, it's only a preview.

ARNIE

Wrong. It's only *your* life. And *my* future.

MINNA

Brigitta is so excited. She says it's wonderful.

ARNIE

At least she saw the rushes. She knows what to expect.

MINNA

You should have been there when they were filming it. That Gundi is such a bastard. Not letting the writer on the set.

ARNIE

A lot of directors are like that. Control… control… control.

(*The INTERCOM buzzes.*)

MINNA

It's Klottie. Let her in.

ARNIE

What's she doing here?

MINNA

She wants to share a cab with us.

ARNIE

You didn't invite her to the preview, did you?

MINNA

No. She doesn't need an invitation. She assumes her way into any place she wants to go.

ARNIE

Well, let her assume her way out of it.

MINNA

Arnie, I couldn't stop her after she learned about it.

ARNIE

Who told her?

MINNA

I did. I let it slip somehow. She knows she has to be on her best behavior. I've warned her.

(*The DOORBELL rings. KLOTTIE, dressed in her widow's weeds enters.*)

ARNIE

All in black? Very chic.

KLOTTIE

I always dress for the occasion. It's suitable for a celebration or – in this case – a funeral.

MINNA

Don't listen to her! You know she invented schadenfreude. Klottie, brace yourself for the worst. It could be masterpiece! This is Arnold's big night. I won't have it spoiled with your nonsense. Now, can you keep still long enough to let him enjoy his success?

KLOTTIE

Certainly.

MINNA

And you will not speak through the film. No sighs, no stage whispered comments, no rattling of jewelry; no noisy groping in your handbag for a cough drop, and once finding it, offering one to everyone nearby in a stage whisper. Nothing! And at the end you will stand up and cheer with everyone else at the screening.

KLOTTIE

Of course I can do that. I've played harder roles.

MINNA

Well then, we're off.

KLOTTIE

Shall I turn off the lights?

MINNA

No. I always leave them on.

KLOTTIE

Afraid of the dark?

MINNA

Yes. I suppose I am.

ARNIE

Better take a raincoat. Looks like rain.

MINNA

I hate wearing a raincoat. It's so... so... timid. Whenever I put one on I feel like a librarian in a suburban town. Tonight I want to feel like...

(A beat)

...like myself.

ARNIE

At least carry an umbrella.

MINNA

It always stops raining when I carry one.

ARNIE

More reason to carry one. That way you control the weather. You really should take better care of yourself.

MINNA

Nobody gets sick from the rain. Come. It's going to be a wonderful evening.

(They exit the apartment together.)

LIGHTS OUT

ACT TWO

Scene Three

(Minna's apartment. One year later. ARNIE, KLOTTIE, and MINNA sit in silence. MINNA is reading a book, KLOTTIE flips pages of a magazine, and ARNIE is writing in pencil on some papers. The downstairs INTERCOM buzzes.)

ROBB (through speaker)

Minna, its Robb. Robb Rhinehardt...

(She sits there, refusing to respond.)

I know you're up there. I could see you and Arnie and some little old man behind the curtains. I wouldn't be here if it wasn't important. I have news. Great news!

(KLOTTIE rushes towards the intercom, as MINNA tries to stop her.)

MINNA

Why did you do that?

KLOTTIE

This old man wants to hear the great news.

MINNA

There is no great news. He's just a shameless boy.

KLOTTIE

(Looking at ARNIE as if MINNA means him)

Yes, *he* is. But I want to hear the other one's news.

(The DOORBELL rings. MINNA opens the door. ROBB stands there carrying a paper bag with a bottle of champagne sticking out of it. He enters. KLOTTIE pulls his ears to his astonishment.)

KLOTTIE

Tell the truth, or there's more from this old man!

ROBB

Sorry, Klottie. I couldn't see that well from the street. Nice dress.

KLOTTIE
(*Showing off the cheap cotton house dress like a model.*)
Balenciaga.

ROBB
Arnie, how ya doing? Minna, you never looked better.
(*They do not reply.*)
How long has it been? Too long! God, but I missed you guys.

ARNIE
What the hell is wrong with you? I told you the night of that goddamned preview that we didn't want to see you again. Time hasn't changed anything.

ROBB
Fuck all, but it has. Look, it's not easy for me to come here. I'm not insensitive. And I'm not stupid. I know what you both think of me, and I don't blame you. Don't forgive! Don't forget! Just put the past aside for a while. We've got a future. A great future.

MINNA
Not with you. I only sold the rights to Brigitta because Arnie would be writing the screenplay. And look what happened.

ROBB
Well, he wrote the screenplay, and it didn't work.

MINNA
For who? For De Sica? Who knows if there ever was a De Sica? Maybe her hairdresser was named De Sica. These people!

ROBB
Gundi tried to be very generous.

MINNA
How? By trashing his script and cutting Arnie out of the picture?

ROBB
I know it hurt but he felt that Arnie's work was too... too... European for an American film.

MINNA
Budapest!

ROBB

You showed her beaten, starved, raped. She just endured, and stood there like a witness to all the horror around her. A spectator to her own life. Gundi didn't think the picture could succeed as just a holocaust picture. So, we had to invent a bit. Fill out the details.

MINNA

You mean falsify my life?

ROBB

Goddamn it, Minna. It's wasn't your life anymore. It was a property.

MINNA

What?

ROBB

When they paid you that money, they owned your life.

MINNA

Which is more than the Nazis or the Soviets did. They merely captured and tormented me.

ARNIE

Robb, it's a year too late for apologies. She doesn't want to hear this, nor do I.

ROBB

Gundi wanted to make a successful film. And if he needed an escape and some kids, and if he had to stick a fucking rifle in her hands, he did it. But I protected you, Arnie. No matter what, you got that credit. Okay, you shared a story credit. Story by Maurice Gundi and Arnold Forman.

MINNA

And the screenplay credit?

ROBB

Gundi and me. I gave it a polish. That's all that movies are. Rewritten.

MINNA

So that was your plan from the start? To use the existing script, Arnie's script, and add that nonsense to it?

ROBB

Do you think I want it this way? No, I didn't But it wouldn't have gotten made unless we did what we did.

MINNA

And that's all that matters? Getting it made?

ROBB

Getting it made is the key. It's the door. It's the way.

MINNA

You didn't need to do this. You're too young. At your age I'd never have –

ROBB

You didn't have to. All you had to do was look pretty and spread your legs to get what you wanted.

(*ARNIE grabs ROBB around the neck and throws him to the floor. MINNA takes the warm beer and douses him with it.*)

MINNA

I christen you the good ship, Budapest.

ROBB

(*Mournfully*)

I'm sorry. But that fuckin' De Sica hated it, and Brigitta wanted it made. She knew it was her last big chance.

MINNA

You're sleeping with her aren't you?

ROBB

No. Ask Arnie. I got problems.

MINNA

(*Skeptical*)

And she cured them.

ROBB

Look, I didn't come here to argue with you guys. I came to celebrate. Arnie, now that I've been launched, can you get some glasses. No paper cups. This is the good stuff.

(*He takes out a bottle of Krystal champagne and holds it up for all to see.*)

The great stuff! For great news!

ARNIE

Robb, get it out and get out. I'm done with your bullshit.

ROBB

We're saved!

ARNIE

You've had a run in with Billy Graham?

ROBB

We've been nominated.

ARNIE

What?

ROBB

I just got the call from Gundi. He got it from some friend at the Academy. We've been nominated for an Oscar.

MINNA

Budapest!

ARNIE

Impossible. The picture opened and closed months ago. The critics hated it. Nobody saw it. They don't reward failure that way. The script was a bad joke and the acting was –

ROBB

I'm telling you *it's true*. It'll be out tomorrow in *Variety*. I got fifty bucks worth of bubbles right here and a cork waiting to be popped.

MINNA
(To ARNIE)

You don't think he could be telling the truth?

ARNIE

He has been known to blunder into a truth blindly once or twice.
(The TELEPHONE rings. ARNIE rises, goes to answer it.)
Hello. Yes. Put her on. Hi. No, I'm standing. Okay, now I'm sitting.
(He waits)
Thanks. Should I be pleased? Well, will wonders never cease. Thanks… thanks. I've got a houseful of well-wishers. We'll talk later.
(To MINNA)
That was my agent. We got nominated. For special effects

KLOTTIE

What special effects?

MINNA

Making Brigitta look thirty again. This is foolishness. The picture is dead. Everyone said it was dead.

ROBB

Except Gundi. He never stopped trying to revive it. He took out a full-page ad in *Variety*, using his own money, with that picture of Brigitta behind the barbed wire, and a banner headline, "Lest we forget!" He shamed the Academy into that nomination.

MINNA

So everything changes?

ARNIE

Nothing changes. There was no nomination for the picture, for the acting, or the writing.

ROBB

Who cares? What matters is the nomination. The little Oscar they stick next to the ad. They're planning to reopen it in a few weeks in some small art houses in L.A. and Manhattan. Who knows what can happen to us now?

ARNIE

Us? There is no us.

ROBB
(Looking at MINNA)

It can have another life if it's properly promoted. If there were some way to create a new interest in it. Picture this. Edward R. Murrow and Minna on *Person to Person*.

ARNIE

There's no way that Minna's going to help promote that movie. No way.

ROBB

Isn't that for Minna to decide?

ARNIE

There's no decision. She won't consider it.

(The INTERCOM buzzes again. ROBB goes to answer it.)

ROBB

It's Brigitta.

ARNIE
(To MINNA)

Shall I try to stop her?

MINNA

No, let her come up. This place needs a good cleaning.
(*Dryly, looking at ROBB*)
I hope she brought some roach powder.

(*ARNIE automatically brushes his hair back with his fingers and rises, as MINNA watches him. The front DOORBELL rings and ROBB opens it. BRIGITTA kisses him on both cheeks She runs a finger over the dust on the sideboard and studies the tip of her finger disapprovingly.*)

BRIGITTA
(*To ROBB*)

Great news, no? I suppose you told them about the nomination?

ROBB

Yes.

BRIGITTA

Blabbermouth. I told you to clear the way. Strew the path with rose-petals. Not spoil the surprise. So you heard. I must say I was delighted but hurt. No nomination for my performance. But what else could I expect from that hateful Academy? They wouldn't know great acting if they saw it – unless a critic said that it was. Still, it's quite wonderful, isn't it?

MINNA

You mean the way Gundi was able to make the Academy voters feel so guilty that they threw some trivial nomination at that... that... that corpse.

BRIGITTA

I can't believe you still harbor a grudge about that courageous film. It's very small of you, Minna. Unworthy of the Minna I know. I only wanted to protect you. Once it's back in distribution, you stand an excellent chance of finally getting some security. You know you have a small share in the subsidiary rights.

MINNA

Yes, I can see it now. *Minna, the Musical*. Starring Ethel Merman.

BRIGITTA

It's your last chance. You can't imagine that there's another rich husband waiting out there for you.

KLOTTIE

But there is! She just has to say the word and –

BRIGITTA

Don't you think it's time she stopped prostituting herself for security? Why, if the picture makes some money she can give up that terrible job. She can even afford to keep a writer.

MINNA

Don't worry about my future. I can depend upon those children I saved from the camps. They are all grown up now. They will come to my aid with their "Minna Benedicks Rescue Fund."

BRIGITTA

Stop it, Minna. You know there were no children.

MINNA

So now you tell me?
(As Brigitta in the movie)
"Hush, children. Come quick! Follow me. Yusselle, take Naomi's hand. Nathan, you're too weak to run so I'll carry you. Don't be troubled by the dogs or the guards. Heidi, the commandant's secretly good wife, who has helped me with my plan, has drugged them. You will live! Minna vows that you will live. I will lead you to a new life and freedom."

ARNIE

Minna, don't! They can't understand. If they did they would never have done what they did.

(MINNA turns towards ROBB and BRIGITTA, accusingly.)

MINNA

You two and your Gundi. If I survived it had nothing to do with my nobility. There was nothing I would not do for a gulp of bread. I survived, not because I guarded my humanity, but because I abandoned it. There were no good-hearted Heidi's, no drugged guard dogs, no brave men waiting outside to save the doomed children and bring them to safety. Goodness may have existed somewhere. But not there. Not for them. Not for me. And it was no better in the gulag. Our suffering does not make us noble – we are just made – damaged goods. Clearance merchandise because some part is broken beyond repair, or just missing.

ARNIE
(Placing a comforting arm around her)
Minna, please! You don't have to explain yourself.

MINNA
(To ARNIE)
To suggest that goodness *could* prevail there, and that I might have helped anyone, even myself, *that* was a crime. No, it was worse. It was a comedy.
(Again to BRIGITTA and ROBB, accusingly)
You took my life and with your lies you made it an object of shame. You turned me into your Budapest.

BRIGITTA
You've been eating too much cheese, Minna. All that pepper brie.
(She opens the refrigerator and looks inside.)
Just as I thought. There's a shelf full of sliced Kraft American here. Little packages of orange death. And the milk?

ARNIE
It's mine.

BRIGITTA
You should keep it out of her hands. Dairy is terrible for women of a certain age. It breaks down the nervous system. All this self-pity is too much Velveeta.

MINNA
I'm sorry that I embarrassed you. I thought you were beyond that.

BRIGITTA
I have nothing to be ashamed of. That picture may not be perfect, but what is? It's a battle cry in a war that must be fought. Memories are short. That's why you have an obligation to help us to promote the film.

MINNA
Oh no, no, no. That's how you got me to sell the rights. I won't fall for the same nonsense again.

BRIGITTA
Nobody would have watched your true story. It was too depressing.

MINNA

Apparently nobody wanted to watch your jolly version.

BRIGITTA

But they would, if you go on the television and speak out.

MINNA

Never.

BRIGITTA

You're a brave woman, not one of those survivors with their victim's guilt, treating misfortune as a mark of shame. You're a woman of courage. Now is the time to use it. You must help us publicize it.

MINNA

No, Brigitta. I will not degrade myself by selling that film. I draw the line at selling Revlon's Summer Rose 45. You might use it to excellent effect. You're looking a bit sallow these days. Come round to the drugstore and I'll give you my best makeover.

(BRIGITTA takes out her handkerchief and goes towards MINNA to remove her lipstick.)

BRIGITTA

You know nothing of makeup. That lipstick is too dark. It's one thing to wear it in a concentration camp, but in daylight in New York, it's aging. Minna, it doesn't matter what you think of me. I know who I am! Any time I wish I could retire into my legend, pull it around me like an ermine wrap, and shut out the world, knowing that I gave it my best. But how can you live with yourself when you know that there are thousands of innocents in those gulags – like Wallenberg – with no Eleanor Roosevelt to help them? Hitler may be gone, but the Soviets –

KLOTTIE

Minna, you mustn't pay any mind to this. You must keep your life free for Doctor Tochtin.

ROBB

Who's Doctor Tochtin?

MINNA

I have an admirer, thanks to Klottie.

KLOTTIE

He's well beyond that. Tochtin is ready. Tochtin is primed. Tochtin is prepared. He's already waited a year for you. Isn't it time to give the poor man –

MINNA

Stop this, Klottie. I never intend to remarry.

BRIGITTA

My very sentiments. You do it once. Get it over with, and then you never have to think of it again. Done! Zut! Gone. Now listen to me, Minna. If you can stir the conscience of the world you must do it. Other holocausts are waiting to happen. You can speak for the dead. And the living. It's your obligation. Mike Wallace, Johnny Carson, and if we are lucky, the great Murrow.

> (MINNA *shakes her head and goes to the door, opens it, an invitation for them to go.)*

BRIGITTA

So you didn't like the film? And why? Because you didn't do what I did? You didn't save innocent children. It's small-minded of you, and shows a streak of jealousy!

ROBB

One show. Just one appearance. And if you don't like it you don't have to –

KLOTTIE

You'll lose Tochtin. The man won't wait much longer. You're still good looking but every day a little less good looking.

BRIGITTA

Klottie, *genug davon!* Her personal life is her own. You must respect that!

KLOTTIE

Why should I? When you're poor as Minna you don't have a personal life. You just got bills and pills to swallow with them.

BRIGITTA

So do the rich. Only more of them in prettier colors. Minna, I'll call you tomorrow and if you agree I will have a limousine pick you up for your first television interview. We'll start small with Wallace, a warm up for the big Murrow interview to come. I've promised no one an exclusive. Your story belongs to the world.

MINNA

You're so certain I'll agree?

BRIGITTA

You're bigger than you think you are. If you don't want to mention the movie, don't! Just tell them about the poor souls living in the gulags.

KLOTTIE

So they live? Good for them. But Tochtin breathes! You're a bargain for a Tochtin. A beautiful, mature European woman of wit and culture who still has her own teeth.
    (MINNA looks at KLOTTIE.)
There aren't many of those around.

MINNA

I have a partial bridge in my right molar section. Knock off a thousand for that.

KLOTTIE

Permanent or removable?

MINNA

Permanent.

KLOTTIE

He'll never know.

MINNA

Enough of this. I am not going to publicize your film. Or marry your Tochtin. Now I'd like you all to go. I am very tired.

BRIGITTA

Good. Sleep on it! Come Robb. We can still make the screening. My limo is downstairs.

ROBB
(To ARNIE)

Hey, Arn, you want to go to a screening with us?

ARNIE

What?

ROBB

This isn't *any* movie. Brigitta is going to a private screening of the new Truffaut at the Paris. She's offered to take us. Better yet, François himself is gonna be there. Brigitta says she'll introduce us.

ARNIE

Are you nuts? You think I'd go anywhere with you?

ROBB

You'd turn down the chance to meet Truffaut? You love Tru –

ARNIE

Not half as much as I hate you. I never want to see you again. Can't you get that?

ROBB

No you don't. You need me to get you moving on. Without me you couldn't live in this hovel off the earnings of a refugee and feel so fucking superior.

ARNIE

You are one son-of-a-bitch.

ROBB

I try not to disappoint.

MINNA

Go with them.

ARNIE

What?

MINNA

Go, go, you've been working all day. Time you got out more. Besides, it's clear there is no way we can shake Klottie tonight. She was once a bother. But now she's a barnacle. So escape tonight before she drives you mad.

ARNIE

But he's despicable. I don't want to –

MINNA

What did your parents teach you? That the only people worth knowing are virtuous? I want you to succeed. And you can't do it unless you learn to tolerate a loathsome little trickster like Robb, let alone a grand annoyance like Klottie, or a self-centered old pretender like –

BRIGITTA

Don't say it!

MINNA

Like... me.

BRIGITTA

You will do the right thing, you know. To think our brave little film might be responsible for saving souls in those gulags. I'll call with the schedule of appearances. And Klottie, give up your matchmaking. This is the new world.

KLOTTIE

Nonsense. Old world? New world? Lonely is lonely. Poor is poor.

MINNA

Brigitta, I won't be publicizing your film. Now go. Go! Arnie, I really want you to go to that movie with them. I'm tired and I want to go to bed early.

ARNIE
(Tempted, but wavering)

Okay, if you – but I'll be back just as soon as the film ends.

ROBB

I didn't tell you the best news. Gundi thinks he can set up a development deal at a studio for us. We wouldn't be specking scripts; we'd be making pictures together. You'd be writing and I'd be producing.

ARNIE

I don't believe it.

ROBB

As Oral Roberts would say, believe and be healed my son.

ARNIE
(To MINNA)

Love you.

(ARNIE kisses MINNA, then turns to leave with ROBB.)

MINNA

I know that.

ROBB

I got to warn ya. I don't think they've put in the subtitles yet. But who needs subtitles with Jeanne Moreau.

BRIGITTA

She'll age badly.

ROBB

How can you tell?

BRIGITTA

(As a warning to MINNA)

Everyone ages badly.

(To MINNA)

Call me – when you change your mind. I'm sorry Minna. I only wanted to do right by you. And if I ended doing wrong I never meant to.

(They exit leaving MINNA and KLOTTIE alone.)

KLOTTIE

Why did you want to get rid of him?

MINNA

I didn't. But it was clear that I was no match for Truffaut tonight. He would regret it all his life if he stayed here and missed that chance to meet a master. Besides, I want some time for myself.

KLOTTIE

(Delighted)

A rendezvous with a lover! You got yourself a new lover?

MINNA

Certainly not. I'd like you to go now. I'm quite tired.

KLOTTIE

If you're not expecting a lover why should my being here bother you?

MINNA

(Angry and exasperated)

Because you exhaust my patience. You eat my food. You steal my clothes. You borrow money you never pay back. You attack Arnie whenever you can, although he has shown the patience of a saint with you. You act as a procuress when I keep saying no! Klottie, you don't listen. You don't learn. And you don't stop.

KLOTTIE

Yes, but what did I do wrong?

(The INTERCOM buzzes. MINNA pushes the talk button.)

MINNA

Who's there?

FORMAN (through speaker)

Sam Forman.

MINNA

Who?

FORMAN (through speaker)

Arnie's father.

MINNA
(Concerned, a bit frightened)

Arnie isn't here.

FORMAN (through speaker)

I know that. I've been waiting outside across the street until I saw him leave with his friends in a limo. I'm here to speak with you, Miss Benedicks.

MINNA

Come up then. Three A. Third floor on the left.

KLOTTIE

Nice voice. Mature, yet not elderly. I like the timbre of it. It is timbre isn't it? A grown man's voice. Something you don't hear in this flat these days. Don't tell me *he's* your lover?

MINNA

I've never met the man.

KLOTTIE

I once tried a father-son affair in Berlin. Father was an exiled White Russian diplomat, the son an expressionist painter; you know blue horses and green women. It was all so Turgenyev, you could hear the twang of a balalaika as you fucked. Neither knew the other was involved with me until I confused the son's day for the father's and you should have seen the brouhaha when they arrived together! I settled it all amicably.

MINNA

How?

KLOTTIE

I seduced the mother.

MINNA

How do I look?

KLOTTIE

Lovely. You always look lovely.

MINNA

Thank you.

KLOTTIE

Not twenty lovely, but Tochtin lovely.

MINNA

Klottie – that train has left the station.

(*The DOORBELL rings.*)

KLOTTIE

He's quick! Means he takes two steps at a time. With a son Arnie's age he's well over forty, but with that run up the stairs, a little less than fifty. Forty-seven, I would say, and spunky.

(*MINNA opens the door to a good-looking man in his mid-forties.*)

FORMAN

Miss Benedicks? Sam Forman.

MINNA

Mr. Forman, come in.

FORMAN

Thanks for seeing me, Miss Benedicks. I hope it's not a bad time.

MINNA

Would you like some coffee? Or a drink?

FORMAN

A glass of water would be fine.

(*MINNA goes to the sink and fills a glass from a faucet.*)

MINNA

This is my sister-in-law, Klottie. My brother's widow. She was Klottie Kruger in Europe before the war. A rather well-known actress and cabaret performer. I am obliged to give her credits to spare you her doing so herself – in all her years of glory.

FORMAN

Pleased to –

MINNA

You won't be. Now Klottie, pick up a magazine and pretend to read it.

FORMAN

Is there someplace we can speak alone?

KLOTTIE

She keeps no secrets from me. You got something to hide?

FORMAN

No.

KLOTTIE

Nothing to hide? Ach. He's either going to lie to you or bore you with his nothing to hide.

MINNA

Klottie! Shaah! Not another word.

FORMAN

Miss Benedicks, I don't know how to say this, words don't come easy to me. Not these words.

MINNA

Here's your water.

FORMAN

Thanks. I am very uncomfortable, as you can see. More than a little nervous.

KLOTTIE

No need to be. I was a great star, yes, but that shouldn't make you jittery. If there's one thing I know, it's how to relax a man. A neck rub, a foot rub, and a little rub in-between.

FORMAN

(Laughing)

Were you a comedian in Europe?

KLOTTIE

No. I was a very serious actress. But I always played Hedda for laughs.

FORMAN

Hedda?

MINNA

Hedda Gabbler. The Ibsen play?

FORMAN

Sorry. What little I know about plays and movies I know through Arnie. Or I should say, *knew* through Arnie. He's been a stranger to us since he met you.

MINNA

But he sees you every Friday night?

FORMAN

No. Not for months.

MINNA

I didn't know that. He said that he –

FORMAN

He stopped coming around shortly after he started up with you. I mean – since he moved in with you, he's only been home a few times, and that was to collect his clothes and some books.

MINNA

He told me he sees his family on Friday nights.

FORMAN

Not for the last eight months. He goes to the movies on Friday nights. Alone.

MINNA

How do you know that?

FORMAN

I followed him there a few times, hoping to speak with him. But I didn't risk it. He would be very angry if he thought I was checking up on him. And I am.

MINNA

Checking up?

FORMAN

Worried. Very worried about him. You didn't know about the movies?

MINNA

No. Is there something else you want to tell me?

FORMAN

Yes, he's a very kind boy. If he lied, it's to spare you.

MINNA

Spare me what?

FORMAN

He's too kind to cause someone like you any pain. He'd rather waste his best years than –

KLOTTIE

Him? Wasting *his* years? It's *her* – wasting hers!

FORMAN

Miss Benedicks, Arnie shouldn't be living here with you.

MINNA

(Dismissing)

Of course, the difference in our ages? That fatal arithmetic.

FORMAN

That's part of it. You've lived so many lives. And he hasn't lived one yet.

MINNA

He's living one now. And rather enjoying it, I think. He's free to go whenever he wishes. Nothing binds him to me but our feelings for each other.

FORMAN

Is that what you tell yourself?

MINNA

That's what I know.

FORMAN

Even if he wanted to leave you, he wouldn't. Leaving you would be like running out on a woman with some fatal illness.

MINNA

Really?

FORMAN

I saw that movie, Miss Benedicks – so I know what you went through – all the good you did – getting those children out of the camp. Amazing courage. I think you deserve whatever happiness you can find in these – your later years – but I am a father. And I don't want that happiness to be gained at the expense of my son's future.

MINNA

You think he deserves better?

FORMAN

No. He deserves different.

MINNA

You don't how we are together.

FORMAN

How I see your friendship doesn't matter. It's how Arnie sees it.

MINNA

I think I know how he sees it. We have been nothing but honest with each other.

FORMAN

And that's why he told you he was visiting his family when he goes alone to the movies? You've never had a child, have you?

MINNA

No.

FORMAN

Pity. Keeps you on your toes.

MINNA

Sounds like it keeps *you* on *his* toes.

FORMAN

I know my son. I know his kindness. His loyalty. He will never leave you, unless you throw him out. It would be like abandoning a friend with a fatal disease. How old are you?

MINNA

Old enough to know the difference between a question and an accusation.

FORMAN

I did the math. The years in the camps, the years since your release. You're almost twice his age.

MINNA

You'll have to come up with a better reason than your obsession with arithmetic.

(He removes an envelope from his pocket.)

FORMAN

How about this for a reason? Read it.

(She takes the letter, sees it is addressed to ARNIE and returns it to FORMAN.)

MINNA

I don't read other people's mail. Particularly Arnie's.

FORMAN

Well, I do, when it comes to my son. It's a letter from Yale. His acceptance to the graduate studies program. Before he met you, he had planned to take his Master's Degree there. But after he moved in with you, he wrote to them and postponed it for a year. They want to know if he's enrolling this year. I think he's ready to give it up altogether.

MINNA

So, he changed his mind. He wants to be a screenwriter now.

FORMAN

That's no career for him Miss Benedicks.

MINNA

You don't have much confidence in your son's talent. I do.

FORMAN

Oh, he has talent. But not much of it showed in that film, did it?

MINNA

Idiots rewrote it.

FORMAN

It will always be rewritten by idiots, won't it? With a Master's Degree in English he can teach, have a decent life –

MINNA

Marry a nice young woman he meets in the college library; have some babies, a future?

FORMAN

I didn't say that. But I thought about it. He's not going to go to Yale now because of you. He wouldn't leave you –

MINNA

Ah yes, my fatal disease that binds him to me.

FORMAN

I know it's asking a lot of you. Let him go. I wouldn't be here today if I didn't think my son loved you. Why he loves you so much he'd throw away his future to be with you. You, who survived prison camps, should know better than to incarcerate a young man. Okay. So it's not barbed wire that keeps him here? Loyalty, sex, or maybe just… pity. Pity is just as powerful – sometimes more powerful than a brick wall with armed guards.

MINNA

What about love? Can't you believe that we love each other? Is it so hard for you to –

FORMAN

Of course I can believe it. Why else would he live in this place with a woman who has only a past and keeps him from his future?

MINNA

So he doesn't go to Yale now? As you say, he's young, there's plenty of time –

FORMAN

No, there isn't. If he doesn't go now, he'll never go. Living with you – or should I say living *off you* – he's got to make a big success to justify your generosity. I know he quit his job at the bookshop, and he's taking money from you to live, don't deny it.

MINNA

Why would I? I am not attached to the idea that a man goes to hell when he lets a woman take care of him. I am simply sponsoring his future.

FORMAN

What future? At the end of the day, he'll wake up from that movie dream, and find himself middle-aged, a self-proclaimed writer without a film career, but with a woman to care for who is far too old for him, miserable in his work, managing some broken-down bookstore and trapped in his own life. I want more for my son. And if you love him as you say you do, you would too.

MINNA

Nothing can keep him from going to Yale if that's what he wants.

FORMAN

You're not being honest. Everything here will keep him from it. Knowing that he will be separated from you; thinking that he will someday write that hit movie, and holding on to that illusion long after it's lost its shine. I never wanted my son to make a million. I just wanted him to make a life. And pardon me for saying so, this is no life.

MINNA

So what do you want me to do? Tell him to leave me? Go to Yale? Do you think he would do that? I don't have as much influence on him as you think.

FORMAN

You'll know what to do. You're a good woman.

MINNA

Anyone who saved all those Jewish babies would have to be.

FORMAN

I didn't want to come here. But Carol – my wife – is sick with worry. She insisted I make the effort. At least consider what I've told you? You'll only end up miserable yourself, knowing you spoiled a young man's chance for a good life.

MINNA
(Sarcastically)

Oh my, all that I've got to think about now. By tomorrow I must decide if I am to marry Doctor Tochtin to save Klottie here. Or promote that dreadful movie for Brigitta and the Jews. And now I must consider getting rid of my young lover for you and Yale. Don't raise your hopes, Mister Forman. I've done all the sacrificing I ever wish to do in my life. As they say here, I've given at the office.

FORMAN
(Near tears, almost begging)

Please, Miss Benedicks. My son is my life.

MINNA

That's a burden he shouldn't have to carry.

FORMAN

You think it less a burden for him to carry yours?

MINNA

Good evening, Mister Forman.

FORMAN

Are you going to tell him about my visit?

MINNA

Of course not! I want him to keep loving *me*; not to start hating *you*.

FORMAN

Miss Benedicks. Miss Krueger. I failed, didn't I?

MINNA

Yes. But you tried. That's something to take home with you.

(*FORMAN exits.*)

KLOTTIE

So, the boy has secrets. Boring, tiny childish secrets, but still secrets. I could understand if he was seeing some young girl – but to go to the movies – alone? How can you respect him for lying about that?

MINNA

I don't know if it's true.

KLOTTIE

Why should the father lie about that?

MINNA

So what if it is true? What of it?

KLOTTIE

He lied to you. That's what it is. And if he could lie about that, what else has he lied about? Come, let me make you a nice cup of tea.

MINNA

What's that about? You never brewed a cup of tea for anyone.

KLOTTIE

When I was starting out in theatre the one line I got was "Come, let me make you a nice cup of tea!" just as the heroine began to weep over some telegram telling her that her lover had eloped with a rich Countess. When I re-entered, I could say such wise and consoling words, with a steaming cup in my hands. "He's not worth it dear girl, you are better off without him." And I say it now!

MINNA

Klottie, stop playing games with my life.

KLOTTIE

I'm not the one to do that. You are.

MINNA

Why should he lie about something like that?

KLOTTIE

The father?

MINNA

Arnie!

(The door opens and ARNIE enters.)

KLOTTIE

Ask him yourself.

MINNA

Arnie? What happened?

ARNIE

We were riding towards the theatre in that limo and I realized that I didn't want to be with them. Not for anything. Not even to meet the great Truffaut. We stopped for a light and I got out. I'd rather spend the evening at home with you.

KLOTTIE

It's not Friday night, is it?

ARNIE

(To MINNA)

What is she talking about?

MINNA

I told her something while you were gone. Something I was ashamed of having done.

ARNIE

Yes?

MINNA

Klottie. Go. The bedroom. Shnell.

KLOTTIE

But I've waited so long to hear this, how can you deny me now?

MINNA

Now!

(KLOTTIE retreats to the bedroom.)

MINNA (Continued)

You sure you want to know?

ARNIE

Of course I do. If you want to tell me.

MINNA

Once I tell you, there's no going back to where we were.

ARNIE

If you told Klottie, how long do you think she'll keep your secret?

MINNA

One Friday evening, when you were going to visit your family, I followed you.

ARNOLD

What? Why?

MINNA

You told me you were visiting your family, but I saw the nervous flutter of those lashes of yours, the way they do when you tell me you've had a good day writing when in fact I know you feel yourself a total failure. I knew you were dissembling about something.

ARNOLD

(Incredulous)

My lashes fluttered. I gave you my secret failure look – so you followed me?

MINNA

You didn't visit your family that night, as you said. I saw you go into a movie theatre instead. The next Friday, I followed you again. And the same happened. Why did you lie to me about something as innocent as going to a movie?

ARNIE

You kept following me?

MINNA

That's what I said.

ARNIE

How many times?

MINNA

Four, five – I don't recall.

ARNIE

That's not like you, Minna.

MINNA

You think you know everything about me?

ARNOLD

This is crazy. It's cheap and jealous and –

MINNA

You lie to me? And I am the one who's cheap and jealous?

ARNOLD

Okay, going to the movies was an innocent white lie –

MINNA

There are no innocent white lies. Only guilty ones. The snow that fell on the gulag – that was a white lie. It covered the filth of the barracks and the uniforms of the guards, giving them a purity they didn't deserve. It covered the brickyards where you blistered and broke your hands breaking rocks and building walls. Why did you lie to me, Arnie? If you wanted some time to yourself to see a movie you could have told me.

ARNIE

Why did you wait so long to bring this up?

MINNA

I was hoping you would tell me yourself.

ARNIE

Why tonight?

MINNA

Because you didn't.

ARNIE

Okay, so I like to see films alone. I always did.

MINNA

Why?

ARNIE

I like sitting there in the dark, away from everyone and everything – and if the movie has any good in it – I get into a different world – not necessarily a better one – but a different one, one that isn't about

Arnie Foreman and his fears and his failures. For two hours I can be someone else, somewhere else.

MINNA

Don't you think I would have understood if you told me?

ARNIE

You might have been hurt. I never want to hurt you.

MINNA

So, how many other lies have you told me? Starting with your claim that you love me.

ARNIE

How did you get from that to there? Look, it's all that dumb nomination. You were fine about the film, and then this had to happen.

MINNA

When does that Truffaut film end?

ARNIE

It's about an hour and a half.

MINNA

With any luck Brigitta should be at home by midnight. I am going to call her later and tell her that I agree to publicize the film on television.

ARNIE

You are not!

MINNA

I don't think you are in a position to tell me what to do.

ARNIE

Minna, be serious. You wouldn't degrade yourself pushing that picture.

MINNA

I'll go on television and speak of my life in the gulag. And all the innocents still held there – the frozen winters – the flies in the summer – the endless labor – building those high brick walls that enclose nothing but blameless, wasted lives. The Wallenbergs and all the others.

ARNIE

Do you think the Soviets will admit that they hold innocents in prison? You'll probably make it worse for them.

MINNA

In other words one keeps silent in order to protect the persecuted? I'd rather risk the consequences.

ARNIE

Don't you see it's all about that rotten movie? The more you try to save the poor devils in those gulags, the more publicity you give to Brigitta and Gundi and that lousy picture. They're pulling you into their Budapest.

(Commanding, demanding)

You won't go on that television show! You won't promote that god-damned movie!

MINNA

I'll do what *I* think is right.

ARNIE

But it's wrong! They don't give a shit about you! Or anyone in a fucking gulag. You go on television, you'll be degraded, just another victim exploiting his or her own past. Don't think they won't ask you about the film. They've got clips they're going to show, and you'll be forced to pretend that you like it.

MINNA

Why are you so angry about this?

ARNIE

I don't want to see you suffer any more.

MINNA

And you'd like me to punish Robb and Brigitta and Gundi for what they did to your script by burying the film? Right?

ARNIE

Fuck my script. It's what they did to your life!

MINNA

Sometimes, my dearest, I think you are too good for this world.

ARNIE

Do you really think that?

MINNA

Well, at least too good for mine.

ARNIE

You're the one who cries out Budapest at every lie you hear.

MINNA

But I don't spend my energy climbing up to some moral high ground as you do to sneer at the world below. I curse at eye level. What a view you must have of all the failings of the pitiful creatures below and feel oh so superior.

ARNIE

You don't believe that.

MINNA

Why? Because you couldn't love anyone who didn't share your oh so exacting standards.

ARNIE

You have just spent the afternoon with a pack of liars, and you're angry with the one person who honors the truth? What's this about?

MINNA

Truth? Is that what you call telling me that you were visiting your family when you actually went out to the movies every Friday. Truth? You didn't go there to be alone. You went *to get away from me!* You didn't have the courage to tell me that I was too demanding, too oppressive, that I was crushing the life out of your life. When was that to happen? How many Friday evenings at the movies did you need before you could summon up the truth about us?

ARNIE

The truth about us is that I love you. And I will always love you.

MINNA

Budapest!

ARNIE

I am sorry I disappointed you by not being honest about those Fridays. But it doesn't mean I am tired of you or our life together. I don't know if I can stay here if you go on that publicity tour – if you sell yourself to them.

MINNA

Not even if it helps shine a light on some pour soul in a gulag?

ARNIE

You're deluding yourself.

MINNA

I was, about you. All you love is the goddamned purity of my suffering. The romance of my disasters. You won't let me compromise that. And God forbid I should cash in on my life like everyone else in this country – oh no, Minna is too noble, Minna is too honest.

ARNIE

What do you want me to do? Pretend that I think it's right for you to run away from yourself and join their circus? You expect me to help you do that? Come, step right up, and see Minna the tattooed lady! Watch her perform on the high wire, straddling the truth and never falling into the pit of bullshit below.

(He grabs her arm, rolls up the sleeve of her blouse, where her concentration camp numbers are concealed.)

MINNA

That's enough from you.

ARNIE

I'm sorry. But I can't fake it.

MINNA

(Seriously)

Learn.

ARNIE

You really want to do this?

MINNA

I have no choice. I am an eyewitness. I must testify.

ARNIE

It's all Gundi and Brigitta. They set a trap for you.

MINNA

But you fell into it.

ARNIE

Me? I don't follow.

MINNA

How long have we been together? A year? Fifteen months? Arnold, I loved you, but I watched you tear up page after page of your scripts because nothing is as good as the script in your head. And when you finally finish one, you can't wait for it to be rejected, so you can prove that the world isn't ready for your great work. You think yourself superior to the compromised world in which people like me live. I am no way as good as the Minna in your head. She's strong and wise and without illusions. I'm not. It may only be Wednesday but it's Friday again. Time to go. The films await you.

ARNIE

Minna, if you think it's the difference in our ages, I tell you it doesn't matter.

MINNA

But it does. I'm far too young for you.

ARNIE

When? When should I go?

MINNA

Now. Just take your typewriter and a fresh change of clothes and go. I'll send your books and your clothes to your family.

ARNIE

You've been planning this for a while, haven't you?

MINNA

For weeks. Only I kept thinking I was being foolish, and putting it off. There is so much good in you. Too much good for me to live with.

(ARNIE is crushed, he turns away from her.)

ARNIE

I don't believe you're doing this. You know I love you. You can't compromise your own suffering.

MINNA

If you only knew. I've been trying to tell you ever since we met. Suffering doesn't make you better. It only makes you cranky and careful. Well I am tired of being careful… with you. And now it's time to be cranky.

ARNIE

What have I really done? That lie about Friday? We can start fresh and –

MINNA

No. I hate your insolent belief that you can make up to me all that I have lost, simply by loving me. Look at me, Arnie. I am just what you see. Not an escaping Baroness trapped by the Gestapo. Or a survivor of a gulag. There is no past in America. We are what we are in the here and now. And I'm just a drugstore sales clerk with a terrible fear of waking up poor and alone. Do you know I am afraid to put my face creams on at night for fear I will disgust you. I am that foolish woman who makes certain she rises early, and leaves the bed while you're still asleep, so you won't see me as I am in the morning, an aging woman, my face creased by my pillow, my hair a tangled mess, a spider's web. Arnie, it's over.

ARNIE

Why now?

MINNA

If not now, when? Next week? Next month? Never a good time to break with someone you care for. Some Friday night you won't escape to a movie – there *will* be a nice young woman waiting there instead and it will cause me too much pain.

ARNIE

Okay, go on television, endorse that rotten picture, tell yourself you're doing it to save some Wallenberg in a gulag. Do whatever you want, and I won't say another word. But don't send me away from you.

MINNA

I'm sorry, but I need a change.

ARNIE

A Tochtin who can buy back the world you lost?

MINNA

Not even Tochtin can do that. But I might not say no to a view of the park, if you stick your head out a side window and look west.

ARNIE

You're tired of working at that dumb job, right? Then quit it.

MINNA

And how do I live?

ARNIE

(Appealing, almost begging)

I'll support us. I'll go back to work in the bookstore and write in the evenings. I know it's not fair for you to be the only one who –

MINNA

There's no going back. I have been less than honest with you. I can't live like this any longer. Yes, I have decided to meet Doctor Tochtin.

ARNIE

Bullshit!

MINNA

Do you know how many wealthy lovers I had in Vienna before I married the Baron?

ARNIE

No, and I don't care.

MINNA

So many that I can't now recall them all. I forget names and the faces but I remember the furs and the jewelry and the villas. It's what I did best. I made rich men happy. And they made me – comfortable. I need one now to ease my late life. I must explore all my possibilities – and you would only be in the way.

ARNIE

This isn't you!

MINNA

This *is me* without the Budapest. Now! Please – go.

ARNIE

No!

MINNA

Now.

ARNIE

I'll call you. We'll talk about this later.

MINNA

I won't take your call. I want this to be over. My key please.

(She holds out her open palm. He gropes in his pocket. Reluctantly, he hands her the key.)

MINNA (Continued)

Goodbye, Arnie. Be well. That was a lovely – screenplay.

(A long beat as he takes in her determination. He offers her his hand, she takes it, then kisses his cheek. She opens the door to the hallway stairs and he begins to descend. There is a moment of silence as KLOTTIE emerges from the bedroom. The two women sit down on the sofa bed together.)

KLOTTIE

Nothing like a clean break. This one was easy. He didn't stay around and cause a real fuss. When I left Shindler, the architect, in Vienna, he threatened to hang himself. I asked him, "Rudy, where are you going to hang your noose in this ugly modern house of yours? Low ceilings without rafters don't go with a good suicide."

MINNA

Shut up, Klottie.

KLOTTIE

That's exactly what he said. You did the right thing. When you stop loving a man, you end it. Kaput. Finis. Over.

MINNA

Who says I stopped loving him?

KLOTTIE

No? You let the father decide for you? You thought you were spoiling his life? Wasting his youth? Ruining his chances? Every bit of it true, still, that's no reason. You want a reason? He loves you now, but in a few years, a young man wants to look at his beloved and see a nursery, not a nursing home. It's one thing to wipe the dribble from your baby's chin, quite another from that of your aged mistress.

MINNA

You do have a way with words, Klottie.

KLOTTIE

I see things as they are. You felt he was getting restless living here?

(MINNA doesn't answer.)

No? Then why send him away?

MINNA

He doesn't belong here. He should go back to school or out to California where they make pictures.

KLOTTIE

Budapest with palm trees?

MINNA

He should be with people his own age.

KLOTTIE

What's so good about the young? They have their own lies, only with pimples on them.

MINNA

But it's *their lies*. Not ours. Did you see how he jumped at the chance to go out to that screening tonight? He longed to talk with someone who looked ahead. Klottie, we are always stealing backward glances, fearful that the past will overtake us and betray us again. That's not for the young. But he's so kind, he's stuck here, and he'll never go on his own. Bless your Doctor Tochtin for saving him.

KLOTTIE

So you did it all for him?

MINNA

And a little bit for me. I won't be hurt again… by surprise. No more Friday night lies. The kind that turn into a girl who "loves" the movies.

KLOTTIE

Now, what do you say to a nice cup of tea?

MINNA

I'm beyond tea. But I won't say no to some brandy.

KLOTTIE

Brilliant! Where?

MINNA

Try that cupboard. Take one and pour one for me.

(*KLOTTIE takes out brandy bottle, pours it into cheap glasses.*)

KLOTTIE

Good stuff. Napoleon?

MINNA

Brigitta. Last Christmas.

KLOTTIE

May I play some music on the gramophone?

MINNA

Not tonight.

KLOTTIE

A little Strauss would be very nice with the brandy.

MINNA

Not for me. I'd like to burn down those fucking Vienna woods.

KLOTTIE

Ah, you've got the Robert Stoltz "Zwei Herz."

MINNA

No German tonight.

KLOTTIE

Okay. "Two Hearts in Three Quarter Time."

(*She plays the recording of the sprightly, rousing waltz, and dances with a pillow that she takes off the sofa bed.*)

Did I ever tell you about Stoltz?

MINNA
(*Wearily*)

You had him in '28?

KLOTTIE
(*Offended*)

Nonsense! I never met Stoltz. How can you sleep with a man you never met?

MINNA

I thought that was your specialty.

KLOTTIE

I toured the provinces with his cousin Ernst, the actor. I had *him* in '28.

(*The INTERCOM buzzes. MINNA and KLOTTIE freeze. It buzzes again.*)

MINNA
(*Hopefully, joyfully*)

He's back.

KLOTTIE

How do you know?

MINNA

I know! You were right, Klottie. I wasn't born to play Camille. No more heroics, no more grand gestures, no more goddamned Budapest. Press the buzzer. Let him in. He's back! Thank God, he's back. Now you get into your coat, and leave as soon as he steps through that door. I've been such a fool. Such a goddamned fool.

> *(MINNA goes to the closet and retrieves KLOTTIE's coat, flinging it over her shoulders. She then presses the button and speaks into the intercom, cheerfully.)*

MINNA

Who's there?

MAN'S VOICE (through speaker)

It's Doctor Tochtin, dear lady, a friend of Madam Klottie. She told me to come by this evening. Am I too early?

> *(KLOTTIE rushes to the door and steps between MINNA and the intercom. She pushes the button and speaks excitedly.)*

KLOTTIE

No, my dear Tochtin, you're right on time. Apartment Three C.

MINNA
(Outraged)

Klottie, I will not see that man. I have nothing to say to him. You told him to come here? That's why you've been hanging on – waiting for your Tochtin!

KLOTTIE

Your Tochtin, my dear Minna. I know. I know. Don't say anything! Weep if you want. He'll think it's the music. I'll do the talking. You'll do the crying. And we'll be safe, Minna. Safe at last.

> *(KLOTTIE looks at MINNA, a bit fearful, but MINNA laughs, a laugh as good as a sob, KLOTTIE embraces MINNA, holding her. They laugh together swaying in time with the music as the waltz plays on and MINNA's laughter gives way to her grief.)*

LIGHTS FADE OUT

Gin Lane

GIN LANE

A New Play
by Sherman Yellen

The play takes place during the Labor Day weekend
of 2009 in Southampton, Long Island, on the flagstone terrace
of the shingle style beach house of Beth Grauer on Gin Lane,
and in the same place the following April, 2010.

CHARACTERS

ELIZABETH (BETH) HAMILTON GRAUER, an attractive, engaging
woman, an heiress with an easy charm, and the administrator of a
family foundation, early 40s.

DAVID GRAUER, her husband, a real estate developer, early 40s.

MARGARET (MUFFIE) PEABODY, Beth's longtime friend, the
madwoman in everyone's attic, 40.

CHARLES EINHORN, Beth's former college professor/lover, a public
television personality, silken, erudite, late 50s.

JERRY GABLE, a business "friend" of Beth's husband, rock solid, 40s.

ACT ONE

(AT RISE: the flagstone terrace of the Hamilton Mansion on Gin Lane in Southampton, New York on a late summer morning. The terrace is furnished with antique wicker chairs, chaise, floral chintz cushions, and large potted plants, agreeable, and flooded with light, offering a distant view of a marsh pond, a wood shingled windmill, a beach and the ocean beyond. There is a canvas awning overhanging part of the terrace with a TV set on a table.

DAVID GRAUER, a well-tanned, handsome man in his middle forties lies on the wicker chaise, shirtless, in tennis shorts, resting his back against a heating pad, drinking directly from a soda can, watching television. DAVID has the build and bearing of an athlete at rest. He studies the television screen intently, holding the case of the DVD in his hands. On the screen we see a montage of a fire-breathing sea monster, dissolving into antique maps with allegorical symbols, Elizabethan galleons and bearded explorers. Over these images we hear a male voice, narrating in an impeccable Oxbridge accent.)

EINHORN (Recorded)

The desire to penetrate the region of the unknown, to probe the unconscious – that is what excited the Elizabethan imagination. They lived on the edge of an ever-expanding physical and mental world. In this world everything was possible. Of course they believed in the ghost in Hamlet...

(The picture on the screen shifts to that of the narrator, atop the battlements of Elsinore.)

...and so did its creator. How exciting such a world was to the imagination – invisible, intangible – yet capable of being sensed, felt on the nerves and the roots of the brain, for the Elizabethans were possessed by the desire to know, to attain power through knowledge. The world of Gertrude's sexuality and the world of the murdered ghost were not separate entities but –

(Margaret "MUFFIE" Peabody, an attractive woman of forty in a loose cotton ethnic skirt, art jewelry and frizzed reddish hair, embraces the reclining DAVID who attempts to push her away.)

DAVID

For Christ's sake, don't!

(DAVID lets out a cry of pain as she embraces him.)

MUFFIE

What's wrong? Too stingy for a hug?

(She picks up the remote and pauses the TV image.)

DAVID

My back. I threw it out playing tennis at the benefit party.

MUFFIE
(Accusing)

What ben-e-fit party?

DAVID

The one you weren't invited to. The one Beth gave for Jimmy Carter and the Habitat for Humanity.

MUFFIE
(Excited)

Who was there?

DAVID

Everyone.

MUFFIE

Who else?

DAVID

Charles Einhorn. Still in the guest house, so there's no room for you to –

MUFFIE

Marvelous. At Bennington I majored in Einhorn. Ask Beth! I knew he was sexy and smart and dangerous years before the rest of the world found him on television.

(She goes over to screen and plants a kiss on EINHORN's frozen image as she snaps off the set.)

MUFFIE (Continued)

Loved that man, hated that series. Big deal. The Elizabethans believed in ghosts and liked to fuck. Who doesn't? Still, just the thought of seeing him makes me want to live again. You can't imagine what this month has been like for me.

DAVID

Oh, but I can, so don't bother to tell me.

MUFFIE

Sweetie, I didn't barge in to bore you with my troubles. I'm here to see Beth and bore her.

DAVID

Muffie, didn't you see the sign on my forehead? No vacancy.

MUFFIE

Bullshit! You've got at least five bedrooms.

DAVID

Filled with two children and an *invited* guest. I'd be happy to call the inn for you and see if –

MUFFIE

The inn is booked. Don't you think I tried there first?

DAVID

Maybe there's been a cancellation.

MUFFIE

You don't imagine I'd come here uninvited on Labor Day weekend unless I was in a bad way?

DAVID

You're always in a bad way!

MUFFIE
(Desperately)

Sanford Kaminski left me.

DAVID

Who?

MUFFIE

That Polish poet I've been living with for the past six months. You met him at my Christmas party. I always invite you to *my* parties.

DAVID

Sure. Fifty, with the droopy eyelid and the limp?

MUFFIE

No! Twenty-eight with the spike haircut and the Guggenheim. Of course he didn't have the Guggenheim when he moved in with me. I called in all my markers to get him that grant. Once he got it – surprise, surprise, he splits! Poets are such pigs. Only stock brokers have souls nowadays. That's why you can sell *yours* to the devil!

DAVID

I'm not a stock broker. I'm in real estate.

MUFFIE

Tout la même chose. You know what I mean?

DAVID

I don't! Right now I'm just a bad back with an overwhelming impulse to strangle you for coming here without warning.

MUFFIE

There's more to you than a bad back. I have always admired your sensitivity. Shows in your splendid fingers. You could have been a great Jewish pianist with those hands of yours or at least a Peruvian rug weaver.
   (She takes his hand in her own and studies his fingers.)
Beth knows how to pick her husbands.

DAVID

Muffie, we will not have you here for the weekend. The girls are back from camp today and –

MUFFIE

David, I can't take any more rejection.

DAVID

Then don't put yourself in its way.

MUFFIE

I'm trying to save my life.

DAVID

And you figure you'll accomplish that by spoiling ours?

MUFFIE

Why don't we let Beth decide that?

DAVID

Because we both know that Beth is too fucking kind for her own good.

MUFFIE

She's my best friend. Who else can I turn to?

DAVID

You're not her friend. You're her karmic burden.

(The TELEPHONE rings and DAVID picks it up.)

Hello... No, Jerry, I can't speak with you now. I have a guest here. I'll call you later... Of course I will. Just hang in there.

MUFFIE

Well that's nice. You called me a guest. We're making progress. Now, who's Jerry?

DAVID

A business associate.

MUFFIE

Cute?

DAVID

No. Not cute.

MUFFIE

Of course Jerry could be Geraldine? Don't tell me anything about her. I'd be obliged to tell Beth. After all, my first loyalty goes to her.

DAVID

Look, we can't have you here unless you confine your craziness to your own life.

MUFFIE

You don't have much compassion for me, do you? Why?

DAVID

You're disgustingly rich. You're not bad looking. You have some talent for painting. And you can always buy a first-class ticket out of any place you're stuck in. Why the fuck you should be in such agony all the time defies me!

MUFFIE

What snobbery! Don't belittle my despair. I can't work. I don't sleep. I've been wandering about the city like a bag lady ever since Kaminski split.

(DAVID is about to put on the television again, but MUFFIE takes the remote from his hand, places it inside the v of her tee shirt, making him a captive audience.)

MUFFIE (Continued)

In my daze I wandered over to the Ryan Gallery and saw that I hadn't sold a painting from my current show. Not one. Usually my lawyer buys a little one, a cheap one, but even Murray didn't do it this time. And next door, at the George Adams, Muriel Whelan had red dots under every fucking canvas, like a fucking case of measles. She started painting years after me. I was choking with jealousy and rage. So I went to Bloomies.

DAVID

Don't take me there.

MUFFIE

This city is in deep shit and so am I! Have you ever walked down the street and tried to avoid looking into the eyes of the maniacs wandering everywhere, and suddenly you catch a glimpse of the maddest face you've ever seen and you realize that it's your own eyes reflected in a shop window? Have you ever –

DAVID

(Interrupting)

Muffie, I know what you're doing. You think I'll change my mind if you wear us down but you're mistaken.

MUFFIE

(Ignoring him)

Like you, David, I have courage. I knew I was having a breakdown so I was determined to fight it with whatever weapons at hand. So I risked everything and entered the store. First, I had to pass through that armed guard of Chanel morticians spraying perfume on the rotting corpse of the Upper East Side. By the time I reached Estée Lauder, my face was so caked with pancake and blush I could have made a decent living setting up a booth and selling from my cheeks. And then I ran into your mother. Want to hear about that?

DAVID

No.

MUFFIE

Forty minute gap in my narrative as your mother and I chatted about you.

DAVID

Muffie, go home!

(MUFFIE lets out a moan of despair.)

MUFFIE

You have no real sense of what I'm going through. It's like my life was a scrabble game and I picked all vowels. Not a fucking consonant in sight. Nothing to make a sensible word with. I turn in my tiles, lose my turn, or I'm just condemned to an eternity of a-e-i-o-u –

(She combines all the vowels in a heart wrenching cry.)

Where's Beth? I've got to see Beth. Beth will want to know about Kaminski.

DAVID

I think you overestimate its news value. She's unpacking the girls stuff. They just got home from camp and I don't want them —

(BETH HAMILTON GRAUER enters. She is a beautiful woman in her early forties. She carries a child's denim laundry bag. She sees MUFFIE, who rushes to embrace her, weeping.)

MUFFIE

Thank God, you're here!

BETH

Muffie. Calm down now.

DAVID

Pay no mind to her Beth. She's only dislodging a fur ball.

MUFFIE

Oh, Beth, if you only knew what I've been through!

BETH

(Reeling it off)

Kaminski? The art show? Bloomies? And now David.

MUFFIE

How like you to know without my having to say – you're positively psychic.

BETH

No. I picked up your messages on my machine. Put your things in the attic guest room. If you push aside the old trunks stored there you'll find a bed and some sheets. Einhorn's in your usual room.

MUFFIE
(Giggling)
Where's Einhorn now?

BETH

He's taking a walk on the beach.

MUFFIE

Do you think he'll remember me from Bennington?

BETH

Possibly.

MUFFIE

There were so many girls throwing themselves at him, how could he notice me?

BETH
(Wickedly)
But you were the only one who sat in the front row of his Shakespeare course in a sheer cotton skirt without panties. You used to stand up and stretch so the light shone through it. And there were the times you lifted it as if you were cooling your knees and –

MUFFIE
(Proudly)
I did, I did! But swear you'll never tell my daughter.

BETH

It's our secret. Why don't you freshen up and then, later, we can join him for a swim. Go easy on Einhorn. You know his wife died less than a month ago.

MUFFIE

I'm prepared to wait the proper period of mourning before I eat him alive. That should be at least twenty minutes. So how was Jimmy Carter?

BETH

So nice. So boring. And a little rank. A peanut butter and jelly sandwich that's been sitting out in the sun too long. But his cause is so good.

MUFFIE

I'll see you as soon as I freshen up for Einhorn. And try to find out who the mysterious Jerry is?

(She exits into the house. BETH laughs, looking after her. BETH picks up the laundry bag and carries it towards DAVID.)

BETH

I know. But what choice did I have? She's in real trouble.

DAVID

She's always in trouble. Don't you ever get fed up with her?

BETH

All the time. Believe me, she wasn't that different at seven in Miss Hewitt's class. Why, in the third grade she –

DAVID

(He holds up his hand to silence her.)

No. No. No. No. It's bad enough having her here for the rest of the weekend. Let's not talk about her now.

BETH

David, you're an angel. I know what an irritant she can be.

(Jesting)

But since you're already in pain, she can't do much more harm, can she? I'll do my best to keep her out of your way.

DAVID

(Eagerly)

So what happened at camp? How'd they do?

BETH

Not so fast. Who's Jerry?

DAVID

A business associate. He called while Muffie was here. As a matter of fact, I've been wanting to talk with you about him.

(A beat)

We've got this situation that you should know –

(She puts her arms around him, embraces him.)

BETH

No situations till after lunch. Having Muffie alight on us is enough of a situation for me now.

DAVID

Ouch!

BETH

Sorry, still bad?

DAVID

I'll be okay!

BETH

Don't be a martyr.

DAVID

Then let's book a flight to Lourdes. If the Blessed Virgin can't heal my back, maybe she can cure my backhand. How was the last day of camp? The girls were so busy they didn't tell me anything.

BETH

It was a triumph! I'll show you.

> (*BETH reaches into the cloth camp duffle bag and takes out some papers protected by a crushed cardboard folder, tied with red wool. She finally fishes out a bright, beribboned medal.*)

BETH

Anna won this ribbon for swimming.

DAVID

What prize did she take? First? Second? Third?

BETH

Finishing.

DAVID

Well, that's great. She could hardly float when she started this summer. How'd Melanie do?

BETH

Best attendance award. Never wiggled out of an activity she hated. And she hated them all.

DAVID
(*Defensively*)

So they're not such great athletes. They're very creative.

BETH

Very.

(BETH opens the cardboard folder and hands him a half dozen drawings and poster paint creations. He studies them smiling, admiring.)

DAVID

You gotta have them framed.

BETH

(Firmly)

No, David. They'll get pinned to the refrigerator door with a magnet.

DAVID

(Protesting)

But they'll think we don't admire them.

BETH

No chance of that with you for a father. Melanie's cheek is still red from where you kissed her hello. God, but they're growing up fast.

(She places her arms around him and looks at the pictures over his shoulder. Suddenly serious.)

You know I'd love them both to marry in this house. Daddy wanted it used for happy occasions.

DAVID

Honey, they didn't know your father.

BETH

They know him through this house. He wanted it filled with joy. And it has been. Thank you.

DAVID

So, when is Einhorn leaving for New York?

BETH

We invited him for the three-day weekend. I can't ask him –

DAVID

Why not? The fundraiser is over. The girls are home. And we could use a little privacy.

BETH

(Protesting)

Privacy? With Muffie here?

DAVID

You like having him around, don't you?

BETH

David, the man's sixty if he's a day. You couldn't think that –

DAVID

I could. And I do. Do you have any idea of how much I love you? And hate him for loving you before I even knew you.

BETH

Yes. But was it necessary for you to throw out your back destroying him on the tennis court?

DAVID

Nothing worse than an intellectual who's a great athlete or thinks he is.

BETH

You're not really jealous?

DAVID

Jealous? Me? Just because my wife had a torrid affair with the guy when she was in college?

BETH

Twenty years ago.

DAVID

Look, Beth. I have a perfect right to be jealous. Your judgment in men is terrible. Shit, you married me, didn't you? Against everyone's good advice.

BETH

I happen to love you.

DAVID

What does that signify? For years I've been so easy to love, I've even loved myself.

BETH

That proves you've got excellent judgment.
                    (A beat)
What do you think of our roof?

DAVID

I don't. Does it need repairs?

BETH

No. We had it re-shingled five years ago. Do you recall that roly-poly woman, the social worker who came to the Obama fundraiser?

DAVID

Which one?

BETH

Small, late fifties, with short grey hair, a sweat-stained sundress, and flabby freckled teacher's arms? Well, she looked askance at the roof and noted that it lacked solar paneling. Then she glanced at Daddy's old Bentley in the garage and warned me about the size of my carbon footprint! Made me feel like a selfish giant stumbling about, sucking up the air from generations to come. But I can't put those ugly solar panels on our roof and ruin this house. The thought of it makes me crazy.

DAVID

You're a saint. All saints are a little crazy.

BETH

Yes. St. Cecilia of the cellulite. God I hate growing old.
(She looks at him, aware of his own distress.)
Darling, I'm sorry. Does it hurt all the time?

DAVID

All the time. But it's not my back.

BETH

Still those San Diego condominiums?

DAVID

It's tearing me apart. I really fucked up.

BETH

(Placing her arms around his shoulders.)
You had no way of knowing that the housing bubble would burst when it did. Not to worry. Daddy had a half dozen business reversals in his lifetime and he always came out on top. I've got to throw some of their camp clothes in the machine before lunch. If cleanliness is next to godliness, our daughters are atheists.

DAVID

Beth, I do want to have some time alone with you today. Just sneak away and meet me upstairs before lunch. We've got something to discuss –

BETH
(Teasing, sly)
Talk? What about your back? Later.

(She exits into the house. DAVID picks up his cell phone and presses button.)

DAVID

Jerry, David... No, not okay. I haven't had a chance to speak with her about it. I thought I'd have some time today, but the girls just got back from summer camp and we have guests. I'll get to it as soon as I can... Look Jerry, don't threaten me. I said I'll take care of it and I will... Goddamn you, don't take that tone with me. I honor my commitments. I always have... No, you cannot come here. Stay in your motel and I'll try to meet with you later... I can't now. I've got this back problem. It may be a day of two before... Jerry, I –

(He snaps the phone shut, angrily; suddenly begins to weep; pulls himself together as he sees EINHORN approach. DAVID makes a quick exit into the house just as MUFFY is coming out. EINHORN enters from the beach. He's a handsome man in his late fifties, wearing a wet swim suit, and toweling his thick hair. He holds a pair of sneakers in his hand.)

MUFFIE

Professor Einhorn, how wonderful to see so much of you again.

(She extends her hand. He puts down his sneakers to shake hers, but she doesn't take his hand, instead picking up a sneaker and holding it close to her breast.)

EINHORN

Again? Do we know each other?

MUFFIE

You don't remember me, do you?

EINHORN

Sorry, should I? You are...?

MUFFIE

Guess!

EINHORN

The affiliate dinner for PBS?

MUFFIE

No, I'm not in television.

EINHORN

Well, that's refreshing. Everyone *is* nowadays. What do you do when you're not playing guessing games?

MUFFIE

Depends on who you ask. I call myself a professional artist. But ask David Grauer, and he'll tell you I'm a full-time volunteer working in the interests of hell.

(EINHORN laughs.)

Big, big hint. Bennington College, class of '78?

(He shakes his head.)

Elizabethan Drama 211.

(Proudly)

You gave me an A minus on my paper on Hamlet's father's ghost. "Original, insightful, but disgracefully disorganized."

(He shrugs, still failing to recognize her.)

Bigger hint. I was Beth's best friend.

EINHORN

Beth had so many best friends. Look, I do hate guessing games.

MUFFIE

Okay, one last little hint.

(She turns upstage facing him, lifts her skirt, then drops it.)

EINHORN

(Recalling her at once.)

Margaret Ann Peabody, Muffie, of course. Are you staying here with the Grauers?

MUFFIE

Yes, through the weekend.

EINHORN

How could I have missed you before?

MUFFIE

Easy, I wasn't invited to the party. I'm just here for the cleanup.

EINHORN

So, you've remained friends with Beth all these years?

MUFFIE

Yes, though there was a period during her first marriage when I wasn't too welcome. Did you know Leon Morrison?

EINHORN

No.

MUFFIE

Actor slash documentary film maker. He spent tons of Beth's personal money making a film of people entering and leaving the Lexington Avenue subway at 77th Street. Just the feet, of course.

EINHORN

A short subject?

MUFFIE

No! Two fucking hours of climbing and descending feet. Afterwards, at the Q and A, everyone was gushing about the important statement Leon had made about class, race and city life. Leon's only concern was that the title *Working Feet* didn't tell the whole story. So he asked for suggestions from the audience for a new title. Always ready to help a fellow artist, I offered *The Emperor's New Sneakers.*

EINHORN
(Laughing)

I like that.

MUFFIE

He didn't. So Beth kept me at a safe distance till after their divorce. But David's different. Truth is, I adore him.

EINHORN

Do you?

MUFFIE

Why not?

EINHORN

He doesn't strike me as adorable.

MUFFIE

That's cause you're still in love with Beth, aren't you?

EINHORN

I think I'll go inside and shower now.
(He picks up one sneaker.)
May I have my sneaker?

MUFFIE
(Still clinging to the sneaker.)
Can't I have this to keep? I'll have it cast in bronze and treasure it always.

(BETH enters, looks at MUFFIE holding the sneaker, takes it from MUFFIE's hand, returns it to EINHORN, and turns to MUFFIE.)

BETH

Muffie, behave yourself. Elsewhere.

MUFFIE

I'll be back as soon as I've changed into something less comfortable. See you later, Professor.

(MUFFIE leaves. EINHORN, bewildered, amused, looks at BETH.)

EINHORN

Is she always like that?

BETH

I would have warned you about Muffie, but she just showed up uninvited. I hope she didn't –

EINHORN

She didn't.

BETH

Good. Well? Did you think it over?

EINHORN

Yes. I did. Carefully. I'd love to help you out. But... sorry. I'm overextended as it is. There's just too much...

BETH

…on your plate? I hate people with too much on their plates. All that bragging about busy-ness. Charles, I need your help, so clear your plate.

EINHORN

Beth, I wouldn't have the time to read all those grant proposals let alone the writing samples. I couldn't in good conscience take on more work now.

BETH

What about doing it in bad conscience? I'll get you a reader. All you'd have to do is look over the applications of the finalists.

EINHORN

Sorry. Really sorry.

BETH

So am I.

EINHORN

I didn't tell you, but the BBC asked me to prepare a new series on the Victorians and I'll need to devote myself to it full time for the next six months in London.

BETH

Six months in England. Lucky you. I haven't been back in years.

EINHORN

What prevented you?

BETH

I had the children late – ten years after David and I married. Once they came along, I preferred spending summers here, and winters in the city. With *them*. We planned a trip to Paris as a family five years ago but one of the girls came down sick. And when we finally had the time, David was in the middle of some new business venture.

EINHORN

Come to England with me next week.

BETH

Oh, but I'd love to.

EINHORN

Then do it.

BETH

Can't possibly. David's in no shape to travel. And the girls start school again in two weeks.

EINHORN

I'm not asking your family. I'm asking you. We could send for the girls as soon as we've found a place that suits us. There are great schools in London and –

BETH

You're being outrageous.

EINHORN

I don't think so. You're bored. Discontented. Why else all these good works?

BETH

Charlie, I asked you here as bait, to help raise money for a worthy cause, and to see if I could get you to sign on to the Foundation's board. That was all I had in mind. I have a husband I love.

EINHORN

Do you, Beth?

(He kisses her, she doesn't break away and when she does she laughs.)

BETH

Funny, you were much more discreet when your wife was alive. And we were protecting her feelings.

EINHORN

Sorry, I gave in to my impulse.

BETH

Didn't you always? But don't apologize, I liked it.

EINHORN

I'm glad.

BETH

Reminds me of the "Dipper Mouth Blues."

EINHORN

What?

BETH

The way you work that mouth of yours. Louis Armstrong without the trumpet and the handkerchief. No wonder I was so crazy about you.

EINHORN

You're still angry with me, aren't you?

BETH

Why would I be angry with you? You did what you thought right. And it *was* right.

EINHORN

It wasn't right, it was just easy.

BETH

Sometimes easy is right.

EINHORN

How could I dispose of a childless, middle-aged woman who was fighting cancer, and go off with the beautiful nineteen-year-old heiress to a great shipping fortune? I couldn't deal with what the world would think of me, or worse, what I would think of me. Minna knew about us. Our affair changed everything.

BETH

Come now, I wasn't the first, Charlie.

EINHORN

No.

BETH

Or the last?

EINHORN

No.

BETH

So we all went on with our lives.

EINHORN

Some of us better than others

BETH

You're not really complaining, are you? How many college professors become cultural icons? Your program, your books, your –

EINHORN

That was Minna. She arranged all of it. Poor Minna. Even when the money starting pouring in from the books and the lecture tours, she couldn't spend it.

BETH

Believe me, there are thousands of people out there who will gladly assist you in spending it. I speak from long experience. My first husband had this habit of mentioning European philosophers, especially Ludwig Wittgenstein, every time he wanted to hit me up for more money for his films.

EINHORN

You're joking.

BETH

No. He flaunted his cultural references like a beggar exposing his sores to tourists for alms. When I refused to support his film habit any longer with my personal income, he asked me to give him a grant from the Foundation. Of course, I couldn't do that.

EINHORN

Why not? What's another bad film in a world of bad films?

BETH

My father set up the Hamilton Foundation as a family trust. That meant we were to provide funds to the most worthy causes and the most gifted artists we could find. And my husband wasn't one of them.

EINHORN

Is that what you told him?

BETH

No. I wanted to kill him, not wound him. I held my tongue and got a divorce. And vowed never to get involved with another artist.

EINHORN

So that explains David.

BETH

No, it doesn't.

EINHORN

What *does*?

BETH

He's a remarkably good man. And I happen to love him very much.

EINHORN

You've nothing in common. Oh, that can be exciting for a while, but the years take the shine off that. Other than sharing a love for your daughters, I don't see –

BETH

We've plenty in common. I met David a few months after he was released from prison. We were both volunteers who went to Alaska to help with the cleanup after the Exxon Valdiz spill. We met at the coast guard station where they were teaching us to save the dying, oil-soaked birds. He was a genius at it. Took to it right away. I saw more rescued birds fly off his hands than anyone else who was there. I said I want those hands to touch me – and maybe I can fly too.

EINHORN

You didn't.

BETH

Of course not. But I thought it. And it never takes me long to transform a thought into an action. As you may recall.

EINHORN

Pretty story. But today? He's just another businessman with a bad back and a frenzy to win. The oil-soaked birds are gone and what are you left with?

BETH

Two young daughters. And a great deal of love.

EINHORN

Romantic love?

BETH

Call it that if you like. I suppose it *is* what we have with each other.

EINHORN

You think that's a state of nature? It's just a modern convention. The Greeks and Romans never spoke of love as we do. Nobody honored love till the eleventh century when some French troubadours invented it to dignify court adultery. A word to describe men and women fucking to the sound of lutes and sighs. It's a cultural phenomenon, born in time, and it will die in time.

BETH

It seems to have a greater chance for survival than you think, Charlie.

EINHORN

Do you really believe that your romantic love can survive Gangsta Rap? Hip-hop? The Republicans and Lady GaGa? No, Beth, the end time is almost upon us. It's nearly over for love as we know it.

BETH

Then why do you bother with it, Charlie?

EINHORN

Because you and I could be so happy together in England. Don't put me off too long. Christ, I'm fifty-five.

BETH

Fifty-nine, probably sixty.

EINHORN

You're a slave to the truth, Beth. That's a dangerous bondage. I suppose your answer is no as in n-o-w?

BETH

N as in never, Charlie.

EINHORN

Poor David. Unlucky bastard.

BETH

Wrong! Rich David. Fortunate David.

EINHORN

Beth, I've seen it happen so often. Indeed, it happens to me time and again. You put a man on a pedestal and soon enough he's on the shelf.
        (He checks his watch.)
I should leave for the city soon.

BETH

And begin the search for my London replacement?

EINHORN

I find it hard to travel alone these days. And good companions are getting harder to find.

(MUFFIE re-enters, wearing her sheer cotton skirt.)

EINHORN

Beth, I promised to take your daughters to the nature preserve in Easthampton before I left. I suppose we should go while it's still light. I'm going to take some pictures.

MUFFIE

Watch out for the goddamned swans. Once they waddle out of the water they are as nasty as Ann Coulter on a book tour with those long necks and angry beaks. One of them chased me and tried to bite my ass the last time I visited the preserve. Not that a little nibble on the posterior can't be exciting from the right person.

BETH

You're making him blush like a boy.

EINHORN

Thank you, I'll settle for anything that will remind me of my youth. I suppose when we get back I should be leaving.

MUFFIE

I thought you were staying the weekend.

EINHORN

A change of plan.

MUFFIE

I hope I didn't drive you away, Professor.
(To BETH)
Amazing, he's going and I haven't even bored him with my tale of Kaminski and the Guggenheim.
(To EINHORN)
I'll catch up with you later, Professor.

(He exits, a bit confused.)

BETH

If you're going to stay, make yourself useful. Help me set the table for lunch.

(BETH holds out a basket of silverware and napkins, forcing a reluctant MUFFIE to help her set the table. MUFFIE puts the silverware down any which way.)

BETH (Continued)

My God, don't you even know how to set a table? Here, napkin, spoon, fork, knife –

MUFFIE

I'm an artist. I take pride in having no domestic virtues.

(During the course of the conversation BETH takes a fresh pile of garden flowers, cuts their ends, and arranges them in a bouquet as they speak, enjoying this act immensely.)

MUFFIE (Continued)

Still looks good, that Einhorn. Such beautiful hands. I didn't count one liver spot on them. Probably has them burned off. You know David dislikes him intensely.

BETH

Did David say something to you?

MUFFIE

He doesn't have to. Just mention Einhorn's name and he grimaces.

BETH

He's in physical pain. His back is out again.

MUFFIE

It's not his back, it's his psyche. I have a radar for spotting troubled people like David. When I see a fellow despondent – that's what I call us, not your garden variety depressives – I can spot a potential overdose in the eyes. We never miss each other.

BETH

Muffie, if something was really wrong, he'd tell me. We don't hide how we feel from each other.

MUFFIE

Did I tell you that I ran into his mother while I was wandering through Bloomies during my futile search for oblivion? "Mrs. Grauer, you're looking wonderful," says I. "Please don't kiss me, you look like you're coming down with something," says she. What she means is, "Who knows where that mouth of yours has been lately."

(BETH laughs.)

MUFFIE (Continued)

Then she invites me to eat yogurt with her at the Forty Carrots downstairs. When she finds out I was planning a surprise visit to you, it opened up the floodgates about the disgrace that killed her husband.

BETH

The man was over eighty and diabetic. He might have died from an extra slice of birthday cake if nothing had happened. The fork goes there! My God, Muffie, learn the simple stuff and perhaps the more complex matters will fall into line. Spoon there. Yes, David made a bad mistake. My God, he was keeping a whole village in Africa alive and he'd run out of money. People were starving. So he sold some company shares that didn't belong to him. If she can't find it in herself to forgive David, after twenty years, I'm glad she won't visit here.

MUFFIE

Trust me, I took his part. I said to her, Mrs. Grauer, it was such a long time ago. He's a different man today. And she gives me that Madame Defarge at the tumbrel look, saying, "It was like yesterday to me." And God strike me down, she picks up her spoon and starts working on the yogurt I hadn't finished. Ravenous old crow.

BETH
(Laughing)
You're awful. That's why I love you so much.

MUFFIE

I know. But why can't other people feel that way. Kaminski told me he hated me.

BETH

It's just that a little of you goes a very long way. You've never learned to behave.

MUFFIE

If I had a house like this, I could behave. So easy to act decently when you're arranging a bouquet of garden flowers and looking at your own great sky, your own private beach, your own old historic windmill. Just another reason to envy you. This house. This beautiful house.

BETH

With all your money you could have bought a dozen houses just like this.

MUFFIE

Beth, people like us aren't supposed to buy houses like this. We inherit them or camp out with friends who have.

BETH

Well, this one wasn't so beautiful when I inherited it. You remember that the roof was falling down, and the gardens were a jungle and the pond was a swamp. Daddy was so old and ill his last years he just didn't have time to keep the house up. But I've always loved it so. All his decency, his generosity permeates this house. I feel he's still alive when I'm here.

MUFFIE

Lucky he isn't. I doubt if he'd be so pleased with you for marrying a Jew with a prison record and polluting the blood of the Mayflower Hamiltons.

BETH

Nonsense. He didn't care about those things. Daddy wasn't a bigot.

MUFFIE

Even the liberals were bigots in those days, Beth.

BETH

You know, people have it all wrong. They think that our marriage rehabilitated David. Truth is, it rehabilitated me. After Leon, I couldn't trust anyone. It was David who taught me how to trust again.

MUFFIE

Christ, he must be wonderful in bed.

BETH

That's incidental.

MUFFIE

As good as Einhorn was?

BETH

You don't compare apples and oranges.

MUFFIE

So who is the apple and who is the orange? And don't be afraid of tossing a ripe mango into that delicious fruit salad.

BETH

Muffie, you didn't come here to quiz me on my past sex life. What's really wrong?

MUFFIE

Oh, Beth, I'm so scared. It's not just Kaminski going, I think I'm in the worst trouble of my life. And I can't see a way out of it.

BETH

You're not ill?

MUFFIE

Worse. I'm broke. I've spent all my income for the year. I've even spent Pandora's school tuition.

BETH

No, you couldn't?

MUFFIE

Couldn't I? I'm being hounded by creditors and I can't even pay my dentist. I have a number ten lower-rear-left pocket in the back of my gums. Do you know what that means?

BETH

You want to borrow some money from me? You with your millions?

MUFFIE

But it's all tied up and the trustees say I can't dip into principal. You know I'll get a huge check next month, so it's only for a few weeks.

BETH

How much do you need?

MUFFIE

Twenty thousand?

BETH

That's a helluva lot for gum surgery.

MUFFIE

How much can you spare?

BETH

Five thousand. Even that will be stretching it. David says this slump has hit us like everyone else.

MUFFIE

All right, I'll try to get by on the five thousand.

BETH

I'll have to tell David.

MUFFIE

Why? I don't want to borrow his money, only yours.

BETH

Muffie, it's all the same now. What's David's is mine. What's mine is David's.

MUFFIE
(Concerned)

You didn't put that in writing?

BETH

No.

MUFFIE

Thank God! Would you rather take it out in a small painting? It would be so much easier on my pride? And then if I fail to pay you back you could be a patron rather than a patsy.

BETH
(Threatening)

You'll pay me back within the month or I'll tell Pandora about your skirts at Bennington. Or worse, all your adventures during our Junior year in Paris. My God, you were so reckless. How I admired you for it.

MUFFIE

Keep your mind off the past, darling.

BETH

Easy to say. I've got a confession to make. I miss school. Or is it just that I miss being young? When I saw how big the girls had grown – and how full of secrets they were – I felt cheated of these past two months. Not that I didn't love being alone with David – when the girls are around he's always so involved with their every mood – they're a foreign language to me these days – but he reads them fluently.

(JERRY GABLE enters.)

JERRY

Mrs. Grauer?

> (BETH *looks up at him curiously, not recognizing him. He's good-looking but buttoned-up in a suit and tie and very well-shined shoes. He speaks very carefully, as if he learned English as a second language, although he is clearly American.*)

BETH

Yes?

JERRY

Jerry Gable.

BETH

I'm sorry. Do I know you?

JERRY

I'm a business associate of Dave's. I'm here for a meeting.

BETH

He's thrown out his back so I don't think he's able to see you now.

JERRY

Sorry.

BETH

You had better call and set up another appointment when he's up to a –

JERRY

He's up to a meeting.

BETH

Mr. Gable. I told you that David was not –

JERRY

Mrs. Grauer. I don't have time for this. Don't have it. Can't spare it. Too much. Too long. Weeks ago all of this should have been settled. He can't. So I've got to. You understand, don't you?

BETH

Not a word.

MUFFIE

I think I do. You're looking for your group? Perhaps they're meeting down on the beach for the speech therapy barbeque? They're grilling fresh verbs and nouns out there.

JERRY

Call Dave. He understands me.

BETH

Mr. Gable, I'll tell my husband that you're here. But I can't promise he'll see you.

JERRY

Had enough with the promises. Need a meeting. If he won't. Tell him I will without him.

BETH

Mr. Gable, I'm not concerned with your needs. I told you my husband wasn't feeling well and I'm busy with my guests so –

JERRY
(Ominously)

Mrs. Grauer, he'll only get worse if I don't see him today.

MUFFIE

Beth, I'll find David and tell him Mr. Garble is here.

JERRY

Gable.

MUFFIE

As in Clark? The actor.

JERRY

Yes, but I prefer Gable – as in the triangular top on a building where the roof slopes meet.

(He makes a pyramid with his hands.)

MUFFIE

Wonderful! The roof has arrived. And it's the mysterious Jerry. I liked you better when you were a beautiful woman and not part of a building.

BETH

If David is willing to see you, Mr. Gable, you can meet with him in the library. But only if he's up to it.

MUFFIE

You gonna be all right, Beth?

BETH

Yes. I'm fine.

> (*MUFFIE exits, leaving BETH and JERRY alone. He smiles at her, looks around, nodding appreciatively.*)

JERRY

Stanford White? Right?

BETH.

Who can say? Every large shingle-style house on Gin Lane is attributed to him.

JERRY

Love those columns. And the corbels. Could be Carrere & Hastings, from the look of those eyebrow windows? But that pediment is pure Stanford White.

BETH

You are an expert on architecture, Mr. Gable?

JERRY

I know a little bit about a lotta stuff. You do, when you got a lotta time to kill.

BETH

Are you a professional time killer, or an amateur, Mr. Gable?

> (*He looks at her, laughs, doesn't know what to make of her.*)

JERRY

You know, I don't like barging in like this. But he gave me no choice. What are they doing? Using a fork lift to get him out of bed.

> (*He moves towards the bar. BETH goes up to the terrace.*)

BETH

May I get you something to drink, while you wait, Mr. Gable?

JERRY

Thanks, but no, I'm A.A.

BETH

A soft drink then? Some iced tea? Lemonade?

JERRY

Wouldn't mind a Classic Coke, if you got one. If you don't, a Pepsi, but I need my shot of caffeine, and I hate the taste of those sugar substitutes. Saccharine'll kill you.

(She goes to bar, picks up can, opens it, adds it to glass of ice. As she does this, he takes out a cigarette.)

BETH

I'd rather you didn't.

JERRY

Sorry. But I figured since we're outside.

BETH

Of my house. I just hate the smell of them. My father was a four-pack–a-day smoker. He couldn't stop, even after he lost one lung.

JERRY

Tell me. I know, I know. I've been trying to quit. Booze I could lick, but this – it's hard, Mrs. Grauer. When you got a lotta stress. My business? All stress these days.

BETH

What business is that, Mr. Gable.

JERRY

Finance.

BETH

Is that how you came to know my husband? Through his real estate interests.

JERRY

No, we met in Danbury. The correctional facility? The prison? We were on the same softball team for about two months. He was a damned good shortstop. That man was fast.

(Looking around, admiring.)

This is nice. I mean, I expected nice, but this, this is… nice.

BETH

Thank you.

JERRY

Shouldn't be too hard to unload it for a good price, even in a bad market.

BETH

It's not for sale.

JERRY

Certainly not. No way I would sell if it were mine. There's just so much property with a view of the ocean, and it's all gone. Hang in there! If you can.

(DAVID enters, supported by MUFFIE. He takes small, rigid steps, trying hard not to hurt himself further.)

BETH

David! You shouldn't be up.

DAVID

I'm okay, Beth.

BETH

Well, if you gentlemen want to have a business meeting, we'll leave you to –

DAVID

Thanks.

JERRY
(Commanding)

Stay!

DAVID

Who the hell do you think you are to give orders to my wife?

JERRY

It wasn't an order, Mrs. Grauer. It was more like a –

MUFFIE

An angry prayer? *Un cri de coeur?*

BETH

Muffie, shut up! David, what's going on here?

DAVID

I tried to tell you before. Jerry and I have a financial problem we hope to iron out. And we don't need you –

JERRY

We do. We need.

BETH

Look, Mr. Gable, if my husband says he doesn't want my presence at your meeting, I –

JERRY

He never said a word about me to you, did he?

BETH

He doesn't often discuss his business associates with me.

JERRY

Figures.

BETH

David, are you going to explain this man? We have guests and I've got to get lunch started before –

JERRY

I don't need lunch. Thanks anyway.

BETH

Mr. Gable, you may be many things, but you are not a guest in my house. Now what is this about?

JERRY
(Gesturing towards MUFFIE, who hangs back.)
I think this should just be family, okay?

BETH

Muffie is like a sister to me. A demented one – but a sister.

JERRY
(To DAVID)
You want to start?

DAVID

Jerry did the deficit financing on the San Diego Dune Estates. There were problems going to a regular bank. You know, if you really listened to the geological reports they would have made all of California a Yacqui Indian reservation. The opportunities were immense. We couldn't pass it up.

BETH

We? I didn't know you had a partner in this.

DAVID

I don't. I mean, *I* couldn't pass it up. I knew there was a fortune to be made developing that property. Views that are worth a million and a half a unit. And there were fifty units to be built. Then, as you know, just a week before the opening, the market collapsed, and so did the cement foundation with that quake.

BETH

But the insurance covered your losses.

DAVID

(Softly)

Beth, I couldn't get it insured.

BETH

So why didn't you pull out of the deal?

DAVID

It was the bargain of a lifetime. The estate wanted cash quick and they were willing to settle for half its real value. If I didn't grab it, someone else would have and –

BETH

If it couldn't be insured I don't understand what value it would have?

DAVID

People take risks all the time. There's no way you can make money without taking risks. I knew we could make a two hundred percent profit on that site. Beth, do you think your father built his shipping fortune without taking big risks? Hell, if his boats sank at sea –

BETH

They were insured. By Lloyds of London. And they didn't! Even during the war.

DAVID

Beth, you should have seen that building site. The Pacific Ocean, the beach, the cliffs. When the fog burned off by noon you could see all the way to –

BETH

I read the prospectus.

DAVID

We had most of the financing in place. My investors knew what they were risking. I told them we couldn't get this site underwritten and they still wanted in. We just needed some finishing money.

BETH

And Mr. Gable provided that?

JERRY

Right. Mrs. Grauer, as it stands now, I can lose maybe ten million dollars.

BETH

That's a great deal of money. I'm sorry about that, Mr. Gable, but you knew the risks when you decided to provide the money my husband needed. You've made a bad investment. You'll have to live with it.

JERRY

No, Ma'am. I can't.

BETH

Well, that's a problem you'll have to work out for yourself.

JERRY

It's not just my problem, Ma'am. It's our problem.

BETH

How's that?

JERRY

I wasn't an investor. I was a mortgage financier. *The* lender. And I wouldn't approve the loan without security. Not even to the best amateur shortstop I ever saw at Danbury. So I got security.

DAVID

Jerry, you're making a real mistake. This should have been left for me to deal with.

JERRY

Left to you I'd still be sitting in that overpriced motel in Westhampton waiting for a call that wasn't going to come. Mrs. Grauer, you knew what I meant by security. I mean, you musta when you signed the papers putting up this house as security... for the loan.

BETH

(Confused)

I didn't sign any papers giving this house as security.

JERRY

No? Maybe you forgot but I got –

BETH

I said I never gave this house as security. The deed is in my name. I own it outright. I would never risk this house. This house has been in my family for generations. It will go to my children after me and –

JERRY

(Taking out a paper from briefcase.)

This look like your signature?

BETH

(She studies it.)

Yes, but I never saw these papers, let alone signed them.

DAVID

Beth, I think we should talk about this alone. I'd like to explain.

BETH

Do. Explain.

(DAVID looks towards MUFFIE.)

MUFFIE

I'll go if you'd like.

BETH

No, I want to be sure I know what I hear when I'm hearing it.

DAVID

You know you've always said that you wanted me to handle your investments. Hell, I made real profits for you. I got rid of all the stagnant mutual funds and I –

BETH

David, I know what you did for me. What did you do *to me*?

DAVID

I wanted to see you and the girls safe for life. Hell, you know what's happened to your father's estate. A whole goddamned fortune dwindled down to peanuts because he refused to sell the ships when they were still worth something. Here was a chance for you to make a tremendous profit. It was my gift to you. Security, so you could run the Foundation and –

BETH

You forged my name on the loan?

DAVID

No.

BETH

Someone did. I wasn't at the First National Trust in the City on August 20th of last year. I was here at the house on Gin Lane. Christ, it's even been notarized. What did you do? Go down to the bank in drag and –

DAVID

Carrie went to the bank with me. She signed it. Hell, she signs all our checks and –

BETH

You had your secretary forge my name on this document? Did you explain to her what she was doing?

DAVID

I told her you were too busy and we needed a woman for the notary.

BETH

What did you use for identification?

DAVID

You left your driver's license in the city.

BETH

Left it, Christ no! It was missing for a week. I thought I'd lost it until it turned up again in my desk. I swore I'd looked there but –

DAVID

I took it.

BETH

But she doesn't even look like me. Damn it, she's at least ten years older than I am.

DAVID

Beth, the notary didn't bother to look closely. Try to understand. I needed the money immediately. I know how you are about this house. So I figured why trouble you? There didn't seem to be any chance you could lose. It was such a sure thing.

MUFFIE

Well, there goes your house and my gums!

BETH

Shut up, Muffie. Not another word from you.
(To JERRY)
What happens if he doesn't pay up?

JERRY

He's an honorable man. You're an honorable woman. Of course he'll pay up.

BETH

But if he can't? You kill him?

JERRY
(Offended)

Mrs. Grauer, what do you take me for? I was an embezzler like your husband. I wouldn't kill anyone. I venerate life. Yours, his, mine, even hers.
(Gesturing towards MUFFIE.)
Violence is not my style. I'll just sue for my money, or this house, and if I don't get it, then I see he gets put back in prison for fraud. Ten years maybe. Could be twenty. You got your grand larceny, your forgery, your second offense. And since he sent the check to me through the U.S. postal – tack on your mail fraud.

BETH

And you would do that to him?

JERRY

Not if you sign over the deed to the house. Then the matter is absolutely settled. It may not be worth ten million in this market, but you can't find property like this anywhere. Understand, I am not a loan shark. I charged him the going rate on my money. But I'm no fool. I expect my clients to honor their obligations. As I honor mine.

BETH

Why can't you give him more time? Why this rush?

JERRY

You really believe that more time will help him? He's had "more time." This was to be settled weeks ago.

MUFFIE
(Raising her hand to speak like a schoolgirl.)
Teacher, if you're as rich as you say you are – and I trust that you are – I can see that from the expensive shirt, the Charvet tie, the thousand dollar hand-made Italian shoes – why you're a walking sign of wealth. So why don't you write it off on your taxes – a bad loan – a deal gone North.

JERRY

I think you mean South, Ma'am. I wouldn't be this rich if I didn't sweat the details. Funny about details – some people see God in them, others find the devil lurking there – but I find comfort in them. Details don't let you down. People do.
(Gesturing towards the roofline.)
What would this house be if not for the details? Just another pile of wooden shingles. Look at that pediment there. The deep-set wooden window frames. And where they gonna grow another ocean view like that with that pond and those birds? Believe me, once this is settled, you don't hear from me again.

(BETH runs towards JERRY, beating her fists against his chest. JERRY is shocked, but DAVID reaches out to restrain her.)

BETH

Bastard!

(Before DAVID can grasp her wrists she slaps him and then JERRY, to JERRY's astonishment. DAVID, thrown off balance, doubles over in pain, as his back gives out again. MUFFIE rushes to support him and he leans on her as he attempts to recover himself.)

BETH

Criminals! Scum! Filth!

JERRY
(Astonished)

Ma'am, you got it wrong. I'm a legitimate businessman. A mortgage financier. A venture capitalist.

BETH
(Consumed by rage)

Dirt! You're dirt. You're a fucking piece of shit. A loan shark.

JERRY

Now I take offense at that, Ma'am. MasterCard, Visa, American Express – now there are your loan sharks. Your excrementals. I never lured a college kid or some poor guy into debt with low interest and then charged thirty percent if he falls behind. I have my standards.

BETH
(To DAVID)

It seems Mr. Gable has "standards." You might have learned something from your association with him.

DAVID

Honey, we'll figure this out and you –

BETH

Just what is there to figure out? You've committed a crime. You've shamed me and the girls in ways you can't understand. You've survived so much shame it's a habit for you, but for me, it's – do you realize what *they* will have to live with among their friends when this gets out?

(She begins to weep, softly, turning her head away.)

MUFFIE

"Daddy's in jail and Mommie's in tears. She lost her house and he got twenty years."

BETH
(Furious)
Damn it, Muffy, this isn't a game. It's my life! Go bother Einhorn.

(MUFFIE leaves. DAVID turns to JERRY in a rage.)

DAVID
Jerry, why don't you get the hell out of here too? Nothing more you can do till she gets in touch with her attorney. You couldn't wait. God damn you, you couldn't wait!

(JERRY starts to go. BETH stops him.)

BETH
No. Please stay. I'm sorry I went at you. Not your fault.

JERRY
No harm done.

BETH
We can settle this without lawyers.

DAVID
I know what I've done is inexcusable –

BETH
That's why you expect me to excuse it.

DAVID
Just need a little time. Jerry will let me have a few more days to raise the cash, won't you Jerry?

JERRY
A few more days?
(Shrugging)
All right, if she needs a few days – a few being less than five, more than two? Right? Three is my few, my bottom line few, okay? Three you got! But where the hell are you gonna find backers in this bear market when you couldn't find 'em with the bulls raging?

BETH
(To DAVID)
Where?

DAVID

Where? What?

BETH

Just what Jerry said? Where will you find the money in three days? If you had the collateral to go to the banks, you would never have used my house, right? So you have nothing to offer anyone as security except your good name and we know what that's worth. Or am I wrong? I know so little of our business.

DAVID

Don't I know that! For years I tried to get you to look over your holdings but you refused. "You take care of it, David. Whatever you think is right, David." I wanted to be your partner, but you wanted to be the Princess Elizabeth devoted to good works and taking bows from your royal subjects. Face it, Beth. Your father was a tough old bird who tried to buy himself immortality with his Foundation. He put most of his fortune in that! And you can't touch a cent of it.

BETH

He left me enough to –

DAVID

He left you garbage. Rusting freighters and stocks that sank like Liberian tankers. That steel drum refinishing factory in Jersey where the cleanup of the poisoned ground costs you more than the assets. I've been supporting you for years now. Do you really think I tried to swindle you? Christ, if the condos had sold you would have made millions!

BETH

I would never have used this house as collateral. You knew that. You weren't protecting me when you did that. You were robbing me.

DAVID

If you can't forgive me, think about Carrie. She didn't think she was doing anything wrong. She only thought she was helping us out.

BETH

You should have thought of that before you made that poor woman your accomplice.

DAVID

She's a single mother with a disabled son to support. You can't –

BETH

Oh, but I can, David. I can. I am not responsible for your secretary's stupidity in going along with your scheme. You must have known that the poor woman was in love with you – and you took advantage of that to turn her into a criminal – like you.

DAVID

What do you really want, Beth? To hold on to this house? Or punish me?

BETH

Both. The house will be passed on to my children. I'm sorry, Jerry, I've decided not to honor his debt.

JERRY

Look, you hate being deceived, I can see that. But how do you think I feel. I came here to get whole again. To complete me. He assured me that he would make his payments in a timely fashion. I invested more than money in him. I invested my faith and my judgment in this man, and he took me for a fool.

(Raising his voice)

I am nobody's fool!

BETH

(Firmly)

Nor am I! Calm yourself. You'll gain nothing that way. We can settle this now.

JERRY

How?

BETH

Tomorrow, I'll have my lawyer draw up papers in which my husband agrees to pay off his debt to you over thirty years. Since I don't expect you to trust him, I am prepared to co-sign the note.

JERRY

What's your interest rate?

BETH.

(Drily)

Best customer rate. No interest. Just the principal to be repaid.

JERRY

Christ, I wouldn't lend money to my mother without –

BETH

You're mother doesn't owe you ten million dollars. My husband does. I offer you a chance to recover your losses; granted – a very slow recovery. Or your lawyers can break his legs. But I assure you, his bones aren't worth ten million dollars – or this house.

JERRY

You're bluffing. I know how you people are about scandal.

BETH

My people can shake off scandal like a water dog in a summer rain. If scandal bothered me do you think I would have married my husband – the ex con?

(JERRY studies her, unsure of her seriousness.)

That's my best offer. Don't hope for better terms. This is the only way you can get whole again.

JERRY

Bullshit! You wouldn't let him go to prison again?

BETH

(Fiercely)

Test me!

(JERRY studies her, turns to DAVID sympathetically.)

JERRY

You poor son-of-a-bitch. You were safer in Danbury.

(Wearily)

Give her lawyer my city number.

(To BETH)

Porch stairs need painting. Scrape 'em down to the wood and use marine paint next time. Something with an oil base. Don't put it off too long. Rot sets in. Someone gets hurt. You get sued.

(Bitterly)

Not that you'd lose. Definitely Stanford White.

(He shakes his head sadly, resigned to his loss, exits. DAVID watches in silence until JERRY is out of earshot, then lets out a triumphant whoop and holler.)

DAVID

You were incredible.

BETH

Was I?

DAVID

You faked him out. Nobody fakes a guy like Jerry but you –

BETH

I wasn't faking. If he didn't accept my terms, I wouldn't have budged.

DAVID

You're not serious.

BETH

Never more so. Not even if it meant you went to prison again. This house is not mine to lose. It's a trust I hold for the girls. And I won't steal it from my children. Is this what our future is going to be? One pathetic scam after another? My daughters exposed to the Jerrys of the world?

DAVID

No. It'll change. It'll all change.

BETH

People don't. You won't.

DAVID

But you did! You should have seen yourself. You faced down Jerry like a mother tigress defending her cubs.

BETH

I didn't change. The present cracked. The past spilled out. And out stepped Daddy, ready to do whatever was necessary to protect his property.
(Wearily)
You know, I can never trust you again. And without trust –

DAVID

Fuck trust. I can get trust from strangers. Love me, Beth. Just love me.

BETH

You have some goddamned nerve to ask for love? After you've dishonored my life – dishonored our children – dishonored this house.

DAVID
(With mounting anger)
Dishonored, huh? What a word – full of old money and old bullshit – it has all the sting of Miss Hewitt's classes – the junior year abroad, the Habitat for Humanity, the arts foundation, the Obama sticker on the back of the Prius. And Daddy's old Bentley rotting in the driveway. Beth, I have loved you for so long – trusted you for so long – and now I'm not worth the price of an old house?
(Furious)
Twenty years together. Two children? And you value this house more than me?

BETH
If you put it that way, yes. This house did not betray my trust. This house was built to last. Unlike our marriage.

DAVID
(Bitterly)
I knew you were expensive when I met you, Beth. But I never figured you'd cost me this much. Not this much. Why is it so hard for you to think of a life without this house?

BETH
You know why! My father died in this house when I was away in college. It's all I have of –

DAVID
Dear departed daddy? I don't buy that now. Honey, you cling to this house because it's the seat of your power – the place where you rule your pretty little kingdom. All the rich and famous come to our benefit parties because of this house – hoping that some of its old world class will rub off on them. It keeps you Queen of the Good Causes. Saint Elizabeth of Gin Lane.

BETH
I have never seen myself that way. It's you who –

DAVID
Poor, old, overworked house. Always helping you to stay on top of all life's infinite messiness. The family fortress to protect you against age

and misfortune. I can't do that Beth. All I can do is love you. So of course I'll lose any contest with this pile of shingles.

BETH

Wonderful! Well done. Shifting the blame from your treachery to –

DAVID

Yours.

BETH

(Studying him)

How far back did this scam go? What did you do? Fly to Alaska after the great oil spill because you heard that the Hamilton Shipping heiress was there, full of guilt because her family fortune was based on ships carrying oil? An easy mark.

DAVID

You don't believe that, so why say it?

BETH

True, it wasn't our tanker that did the damage, but we were part of that polluting world. So this silly little twit thought she could do some good by volunteering to rescue the wildlife. It gets clearer and clearer.

DAVID

No. Crazier and crazier.

BETH

Did you arrange to meet me knowing that I would be so vulnerable to your game?

DAVID

Goddamn it, I had no game. I went there because I wanted to do some good. I do one wrong thing and you've got to scour the past in search of –

BETH

Some past! All the girls have to do is google your name and the first thing they'll dredge up from that swamp is Convicted Swindler.

DAVID

So now I'm the family swamp? At least you could call me an endangered wetlands.

BETH

You can joke? When I feel so soiled. Yes, dishonored by what you've done. I've betrayed my own children by letting you father them.

DAVID

Honey, you've always had a weakness for con men. To be honest – and I am – I'm the best of the whole damned lot.

BETH

None of them would have –

DAVID

Only because they couldn't. I gave as much as I got. Maybe more. And you? Twenty years together and you were ready to send me back to prison? Do you think I wouldn't have moved heaven and earth before I let something like that happen to you?

BETH

Something like that doesn't happen to me! I don't forge signatures? I don't gamble with other people's property. And lives. I don't go to prison.

DAVID

Why'd you marry me, Beth?

BETH

Because I was a damned fool who wouldn't heed the warnings. Everyone told me I was making an awful mistake. Including your own mother. But oh no. With me it would be different. He'd never do that to me. He's a changed man. He loves me, and his kindness to those birds –

DAVID

Fuck the birds. You married me because you were intrigued by my past. Not in spite of it. Maybe because of it. And it would be an adventure. Why, you thought yourself so fucking pure you could wash my sins away – and your own.

BETH

If that's true I overestimated my power. And underestimated your perfidy.

DAVID

Perfidy? Shit – one weekend with Einhorn and you're beginning to sound like an Elizabethan.

BETH

What was the original plan? Get me to trust you so that I put all my family's business in your hands?

DAVID

I never asked to take over the Hamilton Lines.

BETH

You didn't have to. I was set up to ask you to do it.

DAVID

Bullshit! I was doing better than okay on my own. But you insisted that I take charge of your estate. I recall you saying, "Who can I trust if not my husband?" Was that trust, Beth, or a test?

BETH

It was love, or something that passed for it.

DAVID

If we work at this we can overcome it.

BETH

Work at it? I don't work at marriage. David. I work at the Foundation.

DAVID

Okay, you're angry now. You've got a right to be. But when you calm down you'll see that we have built something together that can't be destroyed because of one –

BETH

One? How do I know it was just this once? What if you've been stealing from me for years? Do we have any money left? I'll find out later so we might as well deal with it now.

DAVID

You've still got our city co-op. It's not worth what it was but it's could fetch a fair price even in this bad market. And your stock portfolio is okay. Half of what it was last year – like everyone else – but enough. When the market started to tank I put us in some safe bonds. With your salary from the Foundation and the rentals I get from the commercial property, we'll get by.

BETH

What about the girl's college fund?

DAVID

You don't have anything to worry about there.

BETH

Oh, but I do. I'm married to a man who stole from his father, stole from his wife, so what's to keep him from stealing from his children the next time he's desperate? How are we going to make good on our promise to Jerry without selling the co-op?

DAVID

We can't.

BETH

Then what?

DAVID

We could sell it and live here full time.

BETH

We? What do you mean by we?

DAVID

We always said we would live here fulltime someday. Maybe this is someday.

BETH

I don't want to look at you day after day and see a goddamned thief where once I saw –

DAVID

Thank me, Beth. Thank me.

BETH

What?

DAVID

I just gave you a pretty good excuse to break up our marriage, right? And you're seizing it. What happened? It got old and you don't like anything getting old? You may joke about it, Beth, but you hate it. You might take a closer look inside and –

BETH

Don't give me that goddamned tripe! Isn't it enough you brought Jerry into our lives without now introducing me to Dr. Phil?

DAVID

I'm not asking for understanding, Beth. I'm asking for forgiveness. Why not? If I can forgive you for what you did this afternoon, putting this house above me, I imagine you can –

BETH

Never. I will never forgive. Never forget.

DAVID

Okay. Don't forgive. Don't forget. Love me, Beth. Just love me.

BETH

You're begging. Don't you have any pride?

DAVID

None.

(MUFFIE enters carrying her bag.)

MUFFIE

Einhorn's come back early. Melanie was carsick so they turned around before they reached the bird sanctuary. That girl's an Olympic hurler. She's okay now. A wet towel on her forehead and a cold Coke put her back together.

DAVID

I should see if she needs anything. She probably didn't eat all day.

BETH

Don't go to her now. She can read you like a book, and I don't want her to see the page we're on.

MUFFIE

It's not possible. You're still with him. And he's alive?

BETH

Muffie, I think you should go. Home. Leave us.

MUFFIE

Of course I'll go. But I feel you're about to make a big mistake.

BETH

Not to worry. I haven't forgiven him.

MUFFIE

That's not the mistake. Beth, you don't know what's out there. I'd give up a hundred houses like this to be loved as David loves you.

BETH
(Sarcastic)

Sure you would.

MUFFIE

Okay, one split level in the burbs. But it sounded so good saying that. He does love you and there are the girls to consider. Think what it will do to them. You lost a father while in college and you grieved for months – don't –

BETH

My father died. Quite a different –

MUFFIE

Divorce is a lot like death. When my folks split I figured it was like I murdered their marriage.

BETH

Of course it wasn't your fault. What were you? Five? Six?

MUFFIE

Ah, but it was. Daddy couldn't stand the sight of me because he said I looked just like Mother. And Mother couldn't stand the sight of me because she said I looked just like Daddy. It was the only custody battle in which both parents fought to give full custodial rights to the *other*. So don't rush into anything. Being alone isn't your style.

BETH

My poor Muffie, I've no intention of doing anything hasty. Precipitous moves are your area of expertise. Einhorn asked me to leave David and go to England with him today.

DAVID

That son of a bitch.

BETH

I thought he was ridiculous. And a little insulting. As if I was longing for him all these years. Maybe he saw something in our marriage that I couldn't – or wouldn't.

DAVID

I wish he'd just disappear. The pompous shit.

BETH
(To DAVID)

I wish you'd disappear.

DAVID

Sorry, I won't leave you. But I can't stop you from going.

BETH

I don't know how to leave. God, but I want to, but I don't know how.

MUFFIE

It doesn't take much talent Beth. I'm an amateur at arrivals but a pro on departures. There's always the sneaking off when you're out doing something necessary like having a colonoscopy or shopping for shoes.

BETH
(Exasperated)

Muffie!

MUFFIE

Not your way, huh? Darling, even when everything seems so bad that it couldn't get worse – it gets worse. And then – amazingly everything in your wretched life can change in a few hours.

BETH

Muffie, I don't want to discuss David and me any longer.

MUFFIE

Oh, I'm not talking about you and David. It's me and Einhorn.

BETH

What?

MUFFIE

Einhorn wants *me* to go to England with him.

BETH

He asked you too?

MUFFIE

Well, not yet. But he will. When he mentioned his next big project I told him I was an expert on the Victorians.

BETH

But you're not. He's sure to find out.

MUFFIE
(Defensively)

I may not know Little Nell from Little Dorrit but I'm positively Victorian. I'm the only woman you know who's still a hysteric, try naming another. See, you can't! I weep, I faint, I swoon. I will do anything for love. I even pine away for it. Now who else does that? Nobody! That territory's been abandoned to me, dependent, romantic, fearless Margaret Peabody, Victorian. Besides, he's already offered to lend me the money for my gums.

(She kisses BETH, and plants another kiss on DAVID's cheek.)

BETH

Good luck. You'll need it with Einhorn.

MUFFIE

(Complimented)

Glad you realize that. There are far worse out there than David should you leave him. It's the ones who betray you in small ways, the little daily deaths you have to be wary of. The ones who always remember to put up the toilet seat when they pee, and never forget your birthday – but who forget how to love you. David is the devil you know. And he's such a wonderful devil. Goodbye darlings. Say what you will, there's nothing like a day at the beach!

BETH

I'll see you to Einhorn's car. I should say goodbye to him.

DAVID

Beth, what are you going to do?

BETH

(She picks up the television remote.)

I promise you, David, you'll know as soon as I know.

DAVID

Don't say anything to the girls. Please. Not them.

BETH

What do you take me for? I want them to keep loving you even if I can't. Now take a deep breath, calm down, and listen to Einhorn's Elizabethans. Imagine how these strange people managed to get through their lives without ever trusting anyone, not friends, not lovers, not even God, and still we got Shakespeare and the golden age as a result. Fascinating, no?

(The TV lecture begins. They all stand there staring at the screen.)

EINHORN (Recorded)

(Narrating)

The desire to penetrate the region of the unknown, to probe the unconscious – that is what excited the Elizabethan imagination. They lived on the edge of an ever expanding physical and mental world. In this world everything was possible. Of course they believed in the ghost in Hamlet...

(The picture on the screen shifts to that of the narrator, a long shot of the host atop the battlements of Elsinore Castle.)

EINHORN

...and so did its creator. How exciting such a world was to the imagination – invisible, intangible – yet capable of being sensed, felt on the nerves and the roots of the brain, for the Elizabethans were possessed by the desire to know, to attain power through knowledge. The world of Gertrude's sexuality and the world of the murdered ghost were not separate entities but –

(BETH walks off with MUFFIE taking her arm as they exit together, leaving DAVID stunned. DAVID rises, stares out at the sea.)

LIGHTS OUT

ACT TWO

(JERRY is alone on the terrace, which looks much as it did before, but the table is set for lunch. It is mid-April of the following year. BETH enters from inside the house. She is elegantly dressed wearing heels, and carries a soft briefcase.)

JERRY

Did you find what you were looking for?

BETH

(Looking around)

Yes. You left everything as it was. Nothing's changed. Usually when people buy an old house like this they tear down the walls, toss out the old furniture, and entomb the kitchen in granite. Didn't you have plans?

JERRY

I put off making any changes. They say you should live in a house awhile and hear what it says to you before changing anything.

BETH

And what did the house say to you?

JERRY

"You're a fucking interloper. This house will always be Mrs. Grauer's."

BETH

Buyer's remorse?

JERRY

No. No. No place in my life for regrets. Still, it's a hard house to change. Oh, I could bring on the team of decorators, but despite their best efforts it will always be Beth Grauer's place. I merely *own* it now.

BETH

Yes, you do. And you overpaid for it.

JERRY

You drove a hard bargain. I never thought you'd sell it. I thought you loved this house more than life itself.

BETH

I suppose I did. My mistake. My attorney was absolutely shocked when you bought it at that price. I knew you admired the house, but you could have driven down the price – you might have threatened to put a lien on the house – there were so many things you could have done – and didn't.

JERRY

Let's say, I wouldn't.

BETH

Do you spend much time here?

JERRY

Yes. But I stay in New York most of the early winter until after Christmas. I'm a member of the choir at St. John the Divine. We have our Messiah rehearsals.

BETH

You?

JERRY

Does that shock you?

BETH

I couldn't be more surprised if you told me you were auditioning to become a Rockette at the Radio City Music Hall.

JERRY

I like to surprise people. They get a fix on you in their minds – and it's only a small part of who you are. And if you're smart, you use the surprise in business and in life. So much of my success comes from being underestimated. I wanted us to be friends. Don't think I didn't feel awful about what happened to David. And worse about what might have happened to you if you lost the house. I care.

BETH

So you said in that note with your flowers. Jerry, understand, I'm only here because I needed those old tax records that David kept stored here.

JERRY

You sure of that? If you told me where you kept them I could have had a messenger bring them to you.

BETH

You're right. I wanted to test myself. See if I was up to returning – even for a few hours.

JERRY

And you are?

BETH

Yes, thank you. I am. Well, that business is accomplished. My accountant is still working on the estate. It's quite the mess. I'm meeting with him in the city tonight. So I must –

JERRY

You can't go now!

BETH

Why not?

JERRY

Because I so looked forward to your being here today. I have some great fresh lobster salad for lunch, luscious chunks of meat, easy on the filler. I thought we might talk over lunch. It's a fine day for April and –

BETH

Can't. The girls are at home with their doting grandmother playing video games that are designed to blow up the world, or at least Central Park West and they have homework to –

JERRY

They must be so... so...

BETH

No, they're as tough as rhinos. They had a few rough months at first, but somehow they've pulled through it. It's me they worry about. Actually, I meant to be here earlier so I could get back to the city sooner, but we were stuck in traffic.

JERRY

We?

BETH

Yes. I was driven up here by my friend, Muffie. I believe you met her. And we brought with us Charles Einhorn, an old – well, just old. Weekend traffic in April? And that evil GPS system in the rental car kept luring us on to access roads that led to a KFC.

JERRY

It could have been worse. It might have sent you directly into the Atlantic.

(Catching his mistake)

Shit, how stupid of me.

BETH

Yes, it was. But don't apologize. There's no such thing as saying the right thing to me these days. Strange?

(Gesturing away from the ocean view.)

You know there used to be a potato farm back there – acres and acres of farm land running right down to the ocean. The Kastremski Farm. I'd forgotten that it was no longer there. Hasn't been there for years but I kept imagining it was still there, all the time refusing to see the new houses where the farm once was. When I was small I would pick up the spuds that Mr. Kastremki's harvester left behind – bring a bucketful home to Viola.

JERRY

Viola?

BETH

Our housekeeper? She'd say, "Beth darlin', you always find the buggiest potatoes to bring back. They're not pets, you know, they're pests." I loved Viola. She was so kind to me. Called me "Sweet Monster Baby." She really knew children. She had three of her own. Lila's a school Principal in Dallas and Henry's a doctor in Philadelphia today. Serena is the head of nursing at Mt. Sinai. Thank God they turned out well. Well, why shouldn't they? They had none of my advantages.

JERRY

I wish you would stay for lunch.

BETH

I told you I have friends waiting in the car.

JERRY

Then invite them too. I've got more than enough here and I'd welcome the company.

BETH

Company? You do recall Muffie?

JERRY

Unforgettable.

BETH

And unbearable. Did you meet Professor Einhorn that day?

JERRY

I don't remember. Truth is, you're pretty much all I remember... from that day. Are you with him now?

BETH

No. But what possible business would that be of yours?

JERRY

None. Sorry. Before you go I... I want you to know that this house is yours to use whenever you wish.

BETH

What?

JERRY

Don't look so scared. Not with me in it. Just give me a day's notice and I'll have the sheets changed, and the towels too, and I'll be gone. The bedding and the towels are yours. Nothing has changed.

BETH

And I thought it was my roof gables you wanted. It was my old sheets and towels.

JERRY

Not just for a weekend. You want it for a month? Two? The whole summer? Maybe the girls would enjoy spending time in their old –

BETH

What is this about? You're feeling guilty? There's no reason you... oh, no. You are not serious?

JERRY

Don't. You're too good a person to mock someone's feelings. I only bought the house because I thought there would be something of you left in it. I hoped it might bring us closer.

BETH

I can't say that surprises me. I spotted you for a romantic from the first. Dammit. I could have asked twice as much for it, right?

JERRY

I know it's not my place to ask, but has there been anyone since David?

BETH

It's not your place. And there hasn't been. Muffie thinks I should go online to J Date. And find my next true love,

JERRY

But you're not Jewish.

BETH

So? Everyone claims to be Jewish the way they used to claim to be Episcopalian. And besides, I was married to a Jew, don't I get points for that? Muffie says that left to my own devices, the widow's weeds would take over my life like kudzu in the bayou. Actually, she wants me to get together with Einhorn – since it didn't work out with her. They were supposed to go to London together but it ended after one night.

(Imitating MUFFIE)

"The best one night stand I ever had. Trouble was I had no appetite for so much oral embroidery in my sex."

JERRY

I wish you hadn't told me that.

BETH

You're a prude? Felon, billionaire, and prude. Did the prudery come with the first million? Money is supposed to set you free – but yours seems to have tightened the net on you. Made you almost respectable.

JERRY

Does this Einhorn love you?

BETH

Yes, the way you do. As an idea. Not as a person.

JERRY

And what's *his* idea of you?

BETH

You can ask him over lunch if you'd like. But it might lead to an hour's lecture on the decay of the American ruling class.

JERRY
(Delighted)
Then you're going to stay?

BETH
Yes. I'm starving. And I'm a slave to lobster salad. Sad to say, anyone can have me for lobster salad if it's light on the mayonnaise.

JERRY
My new housekeeper's a local and she makes it fresh for me. No mayo, just a little lemon and –

BETH
Where is she?

JERRY
I gave her the day off.

BETH
Ahh!

JERRY
No. Don't ahh like that. Her kid was having some dental work and she had to –

BETH
Please. Don't spoil the moment. I thought you were planning my seduction.

JERRY
You thought wrong.

BETH
I'm disappointed. I haven't rejected anyone since Charles and I like to keep my game up.

JERRY
I dream bigger than that.

BETH
You sure you want them for lunch? Last chance before your next hour is consumed by Miss Crabby and Professor Blabby.

JERRY
(He laughs appreciatively.)
Sure I want them – if that means *you* stay.

BETH

(Rising and exiting downstairs toward parking area.)

Then I'll get them. But consider yourself warned. Oh, by the way, these days *I'm* Miss Crabby. Muffie is just Poor Muffie. She's between lovers. Be warned. You are so much better looking as master of this house. Was that a proposal?

JERRY

No. But if you'd like it to be, it is.

BETH

I'm flattered. Let me think about it.

JERRY

I mean it.

BETH

So do I.

(BETH goes offstage towards the car while JERRY hastily reaches in the patio trolley for some extra plates, glasses and silverware, and places them with a waiter's precision. As he finishes doing this, BETH returns with MUFFIE and EINHORN.)

MUFFIE

Jerry isn't it? How very kind of you to ask us to lunch. We were starving. I wanted to stop off at a Burger King but Beth wouldn't hear of it. The way I look at it, bad food is like bad lovemaking – better than no food and no lovemaking.

JERRY

And you're Professor Einhorn? I've seen your show. You're looking good.

EINHORN

Yes, that's what I do.

(They wait a moment for conversation to pick up but there is an uneasy silence.)

MUFFIE

What's happening? Say something, Charlie. My God. He's tongue-tied. That could ruin his television career *and* his sex life.

(MUFFIE laughs at her own joke.)

JERRY

Please, everyone. Take a seat anywhere. I'll start with the lobster salad if you don't mind. I don't believe in appetizers when the main course is this good.

(*He takes out a large bowl and begins to ladle out the salad on the plates.*)

I've got some white wine or iced tea – name it, it's yours.

MUFFIE and BETH

Wine. Thanks.

EINHORN

Tea. I'm driving.

JERRY

Why?

EINHORN

Why am I driving?

JERRY

Yes.

EINHORN

You don't believe in appetizers, do you? The fact is I wanted to spend the day alone with Beth, but the only way I could see her was to drive up here with the Mad Duenna of Sutton Place at the wheel. I left London early because – not worth talking about.

BETH

A scandal in the British Museum?

EINHORN

I thought of staying on the year. But I hired an excellent researcher at the V&A and we email back and forth daily. Besides, I wanted to return to the States. I can finish the writing here, and I wanted to see Beth again. The New York Public Library is giving me an honorary dinner in a few weeks. So how could I refuse?

MUFFIE

Ah, we are in the presence of the last of the library lions.

EINHORN

(Assertively)

Do you realize we drove here for two hours and we never spoke a word about David. I wanted to tell you how sorry I am about David. But...

BETH

Not necessary.

EINHORN

...I'm not. Sorry. Oh, I am for you, but –

BETH

Why should you be? You hardly knew him.

EINHORN

Did you?

BETH

Can't answer that. Would if I could. Funny, death is supposed to be the finishing touch. With David, it just opened everything up.

EINHORN

It must have been a terrible time for you.

JERRY

If she wanted to discuss his death with you she would have. I don't think you should be prying now.

BETH

It's okay, Jerry. Everyone was so curious. Why not Charlie? He was there for that infamous last weekend. There was no suicide note, if that's what you want to know.

EINHORN

I didn't think –

BETH

Then you're the only one who didn't. Including me. Hard as it is to believe, I didn't even know that he had gone for a swim that evening. The surf was so rough, only a fool would risk it. And David was a strong swimmer but no fool. I thought he decided to return to the city after our quarrel. I could swear I heard a car taking off in the driveway.

MUFFIE

Bethie, don't –

BETH

"I didn't even look in the garage," I told the detective when he asked me later, feeling every bit the murderess he took me for.

MUFFIE

Beth, please – stop this!

BETH

"So how come you let two days go by and never called your city apartment?" that odious little snot Detective Kirschenberg asked. My God, they were questioning me as if I'd killed him. And the insurance investigator was far worse. He wanted to know if David was particularly depressed the evening he took that swim? No, I lied. Did he leave a note? No. Had we quarreled? No, I assured them. Had he visited a psychiatrist recently? Was he on psychotropic drugs? No. He hated drugs. They sniffed at all the edges of his life and death – hoping that he could be declared a suicide and they could avoid payment. Had he lost a great deal of money recently? Yes, I said, but hasn't everyone? They actually called up people from the party to find out how David was behaving that weekend. When they got through hounding me they worked the police department. Even though the coroner declared it was a death by accidental drowning.

JERRY

How rotten for you.

BETH

According to my lawyer they are obliged to pay out the policy now. The sale of the house to you merely cleared a portion of his debts. So dear David has come through at the end.

EINHORN

You must try to put it behind you.

BETH

Why? So I can keep looking backwards for the rest of my life?

EINHORN

If nothing else, for the sake of the girls.

BETH

They're doing just fine. I hired a grief counselor for the girls right after it happened. Do you know they've gotten grief for pre-teens down to the level of tennis camp or a PSAT prep course? Unity Pope Shapiro.

MUFFIE

What?

BETH

That's her name. I swear it. You don't think I could make that up? UPS – she delivers the goods, luxury solace and easy tips for the bereaved. She said they – the girls – were fortunate to have each other – indicating that I wasn't much of a comfort to them. She suggested that I see a therapist myself. I told her I'd rather swallow a bucket of sand. Or was it shit?

EINHORN

Beth, you've got to move on with –

BETH

Why? I suppose people are willing to believe any kind of bullshit from someone they see on TV.

EINHORN

You mean you can't move on? No chance?

BETH

None. How dare you think I was going to go off with you? Last summer it was amusing. Now it's insulting. What nonsense! Was that your idea or Muffie's?

EINHORN

She's very concerned about you. But I was a willing co-conspirator.

BETH

Jerry this salad is wonderful. For those of you who care, Jerry is my new friend.

MUFFIE

What?

BETH

He's asked to marry me. Or hopes to. Isn't that true, Jerry?

(JERRY nods.)

EINHORN

And you find *my* attentions insulting?

BETH

He's made a ton of money when everyone else did whatever one does to get poor. The world has receded but Jerry has expanded. My first billionaire. I do believe he's richer than you are, Muff. He bought this house for cash. And possibly me. And he did it all from scratch.

MUFFIE

Well, the last I knew you'd driven this poor man to despair. How did you manage to lift him up to the heights of bliss in a few minutes?

BETH

It's really none of your business.

MUFFIE

None of my what? Okay, so he bought this fucking pile of wood-rot and mildew to get closer to you. That means you must oblige him?

BETH

Not right away. You forget, I'm a lady. When David, died Jerry sent a lovely bouquet with a really sweet note –

MUFFIE

"From Louie and da guys." I saw the movie.

BETH
(Ignoring her)

I sent him a note of thanks in reply. He told me that he wanted to buy the house now that it was for sale and asked if I objected to him doing so, since I went to such lengths to keep him from owning it. If I did he wouldn't – or something like that. I told him he was free to buy it if he met my price and then he could burn it to the ground, or build a combo Buddhist Temple and Baptist Burger King on it. I no longer wanted the house. That's why I put it up for sale.

MUFFIE

I thought it was to clear David's debts.

BETH

Partly. David *had* lied to me. He *had* dipped into the girl's educational trust. So with the money from the house and his life insurance, I'm almost rich. Almost. Not your kind of rich, and certainly not Jerry's, but the kind of rich that poor David gave his life for.

MUFFIE
(Indicating JERRY, contemptuously)
So that's your punishment for David's suicide?

JERRY

Who the hell are you to say that to her?

MUFFIE

Her best friend.

JERRY

Best friends don't open a can of worms and then toss them in your face.

BETH

Jerry, calm down. Nothing justifies an ugly metaphor. Does it Charlie?

EINHORN

I'm not sure this one isn't more apt than ugly.

BETH

This – dear Muffie – may be my first *mango.*

JERRY

Your what?

BETH

An old joke between girls.

MUFFIE

Is that what you see in him?

BETH

No. I am flattered by his wanting me. Still stunned by the sudden wonder of it. He could have any number of gorgeous young girls, with his money and charm. *Sports Illustrated* swimsuit cover girls in string bikinis and surgically enhanced breasts. But he chose me – someone he could see himself growing old with. This is superb lobster salad. You can't even taste the mayo.

JERRY

Beth, are you mocking me?

BETH

No. I just have to make sure it's not your charm I'm falling for. I have to think about the girls' future. My income from running the foundation is gone. I had to close it down because the stocks that supported it took such a hit. And the insurance people have yet to pay up. They'll try to drag it out, contesting David's policy for a while longer. When we were children I used to wonder why Jackie Kennedy married Onassis. Was it just the money that could protect her and her children? The yachts? Or the big Greek dingdong? Now I know. It was the warmth. At least the heat coming from all those hot millions. Don't get too close to him –
(She gestures towards JERRY.)
You could get burned from all his heat. And like David, he served some time. I am terribly drawn to time servers.

MUFFIE

Get serious, Beth. You will never... do you mean this?

BETH

Of course.

MUFFIE

I'm all agog.

BETH

Nonsense. Nobody has been "all agog" since 1934, decades before you were born. After that, the world chose to be "amazed." When we marry, Jerry will set up a fund for me and the girls that should –

EINHORN

He bribed you with that?

BETH

Bribe? He didn't know about it 'till now. Don't think it's all his money. He sings bass baritone in *The Messiah* with a chorus at St. John the Divine every Christmas. Man of my dreams. And best of all, he's served his time in prison so he knows a thing or two about a thing or three. I am lucky to have found him.

MUFFIE

You mean you want some guy who sings the fuckin' Hallelujah Chorus? I've never heard anything so crazy. This isn't you!

BETH

It's me *now*. A.D. After David. That son-of-a bitch. Most men run off with a young nubile blonde and leave you reeling in your middle age. My husband ran off with a fucking ocean.

(Wistfully, then angrily)

Before David, I thought of myself as a thoroughly good person. One of the world's caretakers – leaping into good works with balletic grace – sponsor of ghetto schools – muse of struggling artists – ready to be the donor of a kidney or a summer camp for a poor child. What a fraud I was. Am.

(She turns her head away, unwilling to show her tears as JERRY blocks her way, places an arm around her.)

JERRY

Beth, it's okay to –

BETH

(Taking his pocket handkerchief and blowing her nose in it.)

No. Don't stop me, I'm loving this. That goddamned grief counselor stopped up my tears. She kept thrusting this huge blue box of Kleenex in my lap in the hope that I'd break down in front of her and the girls and be a role model for them. Finally, she changed from the big two hundred count vertical ones to the square puff-up ones – hoping that their lady-like shape would tempt me into the big boo-hoo. Finally, in desperation she left a little purse sized packet on the table beside me. I tricked her. I pulled out a paper tissue and as she beamed approval I blew my nose in it. But I didn't give up one fucking tear to her. Time may not heal everything, but money – ah that's something else. Why, I could get married in this house, just as Daddy wanted. Sadly, David and I used the City Hall registry, but I'm ready for the big wedding.

EINHORN

This would be tragic if it weren't so absurd. You can't be serious about marrying this man just to regain this house. What an example for the girls. You degrade yourself if you do that.

EINHORN (Continued)
(To JERRY)

Nothing personal, but the notion of her spending the rest of her life with you insults the mind.

JERRY

Whose mind, Professor? Yours?

EINHORN

What is this, Beth? Some form of primitive punishment for David's death? Sati or, if you prefer, Sutee – immolating yourself on your husband's funeral pyre. That's all the heat I see coming from him. And you, a woman of breeding –

BETH

Jerry, sock him.

JERRY

Beth?

BETH

I said sock him. Beat the smugness out of him. And if you can't do that, just beat the shit out of him. If you don't, I will. How dare he call me a woman of breeding?

JERRY

You want me to assault him?

BETH

Yes. It would mean so much more to me than your singing in The Meshugah.

JERRY

Okay. Whatever you say, babe.

EINHORN

You may enjoy this nonsense, but I –

(JERRY strikes EINHORN and he stumbles backwards, falling into BETH's arms. She drops him as he falls to the ground, slaps her hands in satisfaction.)

BETH

Well done.

EINHORN

I am going to call the police now. We'll see what the court thinks of this assault. I'm sure that as a former felon, he's violated some –

(He removes his cellphone from his pocket as he scrambles to his feet.)

BETH

Try it and I'll call *The Times* and expose you for the feeble little fraud you are.

MUFFIE

What kind of threat is that?

BETH

Charlie knows just what I mean.

EINHORN

I'm afraid I don't.

BETH

Don't add fresh lies to stale sins, Charlie.
(To MUFFIE)
When we were at Bennington, Charlie had a particularly brilliant scholarship student, Lupita Gomez. You remember Lupita?

MUFFIE

Sure, the mono-brow from the South Bronx. Half black, half Puerto Rican, all angry.

BETH

She wrote the most remarkable senior thesis on the supernatural and the Elizabethans, and then up and died. A drug overdose during school break. Lupita's paper stayed in Charlie's drawer until years later when he used it as the basis for his series. He even had me retype it for him when I was his student-slash-lover. Now you tell me? What's worse? That my Jerry here paid for his crimes or that Charlie here stole the work of a poor dead girl for his own fame and profit. And got away with it.

EINHORN

You could never prove it.

BETH

I wouldn't have to. The accusation alone – coming from me – a woman of breeding and a member of the college board of trustees –would be enough to spread a stain over your life and career. Besides, what other works of yours have indicated anything other than mediocrity?

EINHORN

I never meant to call the police on him.

BETH

Yes, you did. And I meant to report your crime to the college, and the papers. Still may. Tell him about me, Jerry. You've made a study of me, I believe.

JERRY

I knew she was what I wanted first time I saw her. I looked at her and thought, "Nobody ever gave that woman a decent chance." Even when she beat me over the house, acting so strong and superior, I knew I could have fought her to a draw, but I wanted her to win. What a power that is. Making people want you to win, against yourself.

MUFFIE

I didn't take you for a pushover.

JERRY

When it comes to this woman, I am. If she asks, I will give up cigarettes for her. I didn't know then about her father dying of lung cancer and leaving her with only a crabby old aunt to look after her. No wonder she fell for Professor Blabby. Even David didn't know what he had or he wouldn't have risked it all, and when he knew what he'd lost, he lost it.

EINHORN

Ah, the romance of a good suicide.

JERRY

No, you little prick, David went for a swim to refresh himself! He was an athlete. Athlete's swim in rough waters. Not like some I know whose idea of exercise is lifting a paper from a dead girl's file.

BETH

Thank you, Jerry. But I don't need any more help from you. My father taught me to fight my own battles.

MUFFIE

Well, I for one have had enough of your nonsense. When in doubt, pull out Daddy. Santa, plus Roosevelt – with just a touch of Gandhi, and a dash of Polanski.

BETH

What are you talking about?

MUFFIE

Your saintly father. I am so sick of that fucking father of yours. You know the old man made a pass at me when I was fourteen?

BETH

I thought that was your father –

MUFFIE

You want the truth? Okay. I was only thirteen. I added a year to spare your feelings. Even Viola would find an excuse for staying in the room when I was there with him. But that's not the worst of it. Rumor had it that before the war broke out – long before we were even born – he was using his freighters to ship steel to the Germans for their war machine. All done under Liberian flags of convenience with the money funneled through a Dutch holding company. Oh, he wasn't alone in it. Prescott Bush, Averill Harriman, all those future patriots were doing it.

BETH

Next thing I know you'll be accusing him of being the second shooter on the grassy knoll.

MUFFIE

Good try, Beth. When faced with an uncomfortable truth, introduce a note of the absurd to discredit it. Done it myself for years. Why, everyone knew about your Daddy. Even David did, and he tried to spare you that bit of family history. I'd like to think that we became best friends because we were drawn to each other. No. I was your best friend because none of the other parents would let their children play in your apartment when your father was alive. Don't get all in a huff. It's not that my family fortune is so clean. Find me a strip mine, a slag heap, or an industrial waste dump – and we planted our flag on it. There's a drop of cyanide in every big fortune. Yours just has a little pedophilia and treason tossed in.

EINHORN
Beth, even I've heard the stories of his prewar activities. Kenson, you recall Kenson don't you? Taught modern history at college. Told me about your father when you arrived as a freshman. It was common knowledge. You, my best researcher? Surely you could connect the dots?

BETH
What dots? If any of this were true, David would have told me. He had all the old records from the shipping line. He would have come back at me that last day with all of this. He would have used it to justify his own –

MUFFIE
No. David loved you too much to tell you what you already knew.

BETH
But I didn't know!

MUFFIE
Of course you knew. And he knew that you knew. But he tried to spare you knowing what you knew.

BETH
Why are they doing this to me? My father gave a half million dollars to the Civil Rights movement when a half million was a great fortune. I found a letter from Martin Luther King himself thanking him. And the cancelled check. He took no credit for that.

JERRY
Honey, even if what they say is true, you didn't commit his crimes. I'm not saying that your father was –

BETH
How could he do what they say he did, and still leave a small fortune to the NAACP in his will? Yes, I heard a few rumors. I never believed them until David died, and then I began to understand how people can be so good and so wicked at the same time.

MUFFIE
David was weak but he wasn't wicked. Don't –

BETH
It wasn't him. It was me. Weak and wicked. I killed David.

JERRY

Beth, don't say that. If anyone killed him it was me. I bulldozed my way in here and set the whole goddamned tragedy in motion. Don't think I haven't thought about it long and hard and regretted every –

BETH

Jerry, that won't wash with me. I know what I did. One word from me, "disappear" and he disappeared. It wasn't suicide. It was murder.

MUFFIE

Bullshit. Now stop this at once! Sorry to bring up all that stuff about Daddy, but somehow I thought it would bring you to your senses about...

(Indicating JERRY)

...that one. Remember, you're Beth, I'm Muffie. I own crazy. Not only do I own it, I hold the patent on crazy, together with my great grandfather's plastics formula. I'll let you borrow a little crazy until the mourning period is over, just enough to get you through the year, but I won't let you take crazy from me forever just because you're grieving. I'm the one who finds the wrong men and parades my fears and my fantasies to anyone who will watch and listen. Not you.

BETH

David died because I sent him out into that ocean to die.

JERRY

Honey, don't.

MUFFIE

Honey-dew.

JERRY

What?

MUFFIE

Reminds me to stop off at the Farmer's Market for melons on the way home.

JERRY

Beth, please. Tell them to go now. I'll drive you back.

BETH

No, Jerry, not yet. I want all of you to know.

MUFFIE

Spare us the entire Colombo rerun. Get right to the big Aha!

BETH

(Ignoring her)

I saw the car in the driveway a half-hour after he went missing. I told myself he went for a walk. And then, when he failed to show up for dinner, I told myself he had taken a long walk to the village and was dining out alone.

JERRY

Anyone might have thought that.

BETH

But I wasn't anyone. I was his wife. It should have been clear that he –

MUFFIE

Nothing is clear. Nor will it ever be. No note. No threat. And as far as he knew, you'd forgive him in the morning. That's what I thought.

BETH

Would I? I'd like to think so now. It would have been so easy to forgive him when forgiving mattered. How simple to say, "Okay, it's done. Over. We'll get through this and go on together," but no, I couldn't. I didn't. It was this wretched house driving me on. I beat him with it until he had no choice but to sink... or swim... and he sank.

MUFFIE

So you have to punish yourself with that one?

(She indicates JERRY.)

BETH

No. You don't get it. He's what I *need* after what I've done. He'll keep me alive, lock the medicine cabinet when I'm feeling blue and –

MUFFIE

(Outraged)

So now *you're* the suicidal one? Thief!

BETH

But every time I got serious about doing it, I thought of the girls. One parent's suicide is bad enough but two – they couldn't help but feel so abandoned – as I did when my father killed *himself.*

MUFFIE

He didn't kill himself. He died smiling in his sleep with a boner pointing towards heaven in his semen-stained silk, Brooks Brothers pajamas like all evil old men do.

BETH

With one empty bottle of scotch and three empty bottles of pills beside his bed? He had the excuse of being old and sick, and sleepless. No. I can't do that to them. I am sentenced to live. You know why people kill themselves?

MUFFIE

They're scared of tomorrow.

BETH

Scared that tomorrow will be just like today. You know I had to identify David's body. His eyes, David's beautiful eyes were gone, and his skin and nose had been gnawed on by – oh, God! It was so awful.

JERRY

Please – don't –

BETH

He had the wedding ring on the remains of his finger. After seeing that, I started to think that only my own death would blot out that image forever. That without my dying I'd have his corpse imprinted on my brain. So tempting. So easy to break free by dying.

MUFFIE

This is too much! It's bad enough you try to steal my crazy but now you're after my self-destruction as well? You are trespassing on my desperation rights and I won't allow that. Not even for my best friend. You're joking about Jerry, right?

BETH

No.

MUFFIE

But Jerry is my kind of bad choice, not yours! He's my mistake!

JERRY

I am nobody's mistake. Absolutely nuts. Right?

(He turns to EINHORN for affirmation.)

EINHORN
No.

JERRY
You're serious?

EINHORN
If I tell you this is normal for them, do you try to kill me again?

JERRY
No. Killing wasn't my intention. Silencing was.

EINHORN
Then take a close look at these women. Part of our great national secret. Class in America. Once you're born into it, you can get away with nearly anything. Inappropriate words, inappropriate sex, inappropriate grief –

MUFFIE
What are you talking about? It can't be *appropriate* sex and still be sex.

BETH
That's quite enough from you Muffie.

MUFFIE
Beth, you sound just like Mrs. Frawley in Middle School. "Put this nonsense behind you, Missy… playground days are over…"

BETH
"….we are here to learn." And I've learned. Dear Jerry. What a coward I am. How brave of you to love me. You do love me, right? All that lobster salad and house lending was love, wasn't it? I am so unworthy of your truffles –

(She begins to weep. JERRY places a comforting arm around her. She allows herself to be embraced by him, burying her head in his chest.)

MUFFIE
Enjoy it while it lasts. She'll never marry you. Comes the great day when she decides to stop all this gnashing of teeth and rending of garments and becomes Beth again, it's bye-bye Jerry. On to the next tasty apple.

BETH

She's babbling on as usual. Don't pay any attention to –

MUFFIE

You're far richer than David was, Jerry. I may call you Jerry, right?

JERRY

No. My name in your mouth sounds like a curse.

MUFFIE

Okay, you're much more resourceful that he was... Jerry. Even I can see that. And just as attractive in your let's-fuck-standing-up-against-the-wall sort of way. But you're apples from the same barrel as David. Idolaters. She's had that. We don't bite into the same apple twice. Not for long. We thrive on the taste of different varieties.

JERRY

What the hell are you talking about?

MUFFIE

If we tire of a Golden Delicious we seek the comfort of a Granny Smith. Right, Beth? You remember, don't play dumb. Play the apple game.

BETH

And when Granny bores us we sail to the orient and nibble on a Fuji.

MUFFIE

Feeling festive?

BETH

Go for a Gala. Kim Philby?

MUFFIE

I know, I know. It's on the tip of my clitoris. Hint. Hint.

BETH

Stealing state secrets like Guy Burgess?

MUFFIE

My dear, try a Red Spy. Feeling all French and fancy?

BETH

Muscat de Bernay. And when all is lost and we turn to the mother church for salvation we bake a juicy...

MUFFIE and BETH

(Together)

Rome!

(Laughing, they fall into each other's arms.)

JERRY

Apples? Beth, this woman is hazardous to your health.

MUFFIE

Apples. All you have to know is one thing well and you own the whole world. And Charlie, it's me, an English professor. And if it isn't, it should be.

(BETH breaks from MUFFIE, turns to JERRY.)

BETH

Jerry, don't mind us. It's just one of the games we used to play when we were girls. We tried it with pears and tomatoes too, but apples worked best. There are a thousand different apples and we would try to – oh, it's not worth talking about. Really, it's only a child's game. Do you know we've never kissed? May I?

(She kisses him.)

Very nice. You are so much more than an ex-con with a love for old houses and despairing widows. But you must give me some time to think about us.

JERRY

Sure. But not too long. I can stand here loving you while you are thinking me into oblivion. Promise me you won't do that?

BETH

No promises. No broken promises. But that was a lovely kiss.

MUFFIE

Gentlemen, if you don't mind I'd like to speak with Beth alone. A personal matter. Won't take more than a few minutes–but I mean alone.

JERRY

Beth?

BETH

Yes, it's okay. Show Charlie around the grounds. Teach him the Hallelujah Chorus. Or play a game of quoits. There's a set in the garage. Anything, but leave us for a few minutes. Muffie and I need time together. Charlie, if I was cruel – well – I had to stop you. I'll never tell on you. We learned not to tattle in Miss Hewitt's classes.

(She kisses his cheek.)

Jerry. This may take us longer than I planned.

JERRY

You can start your weekends now, if you want.

BETH

No, but I may be tempted soon. Let me see what the girls are up to – if they'd like to come for next weekend. But only if you stay on – as our host. They should get to know you. They've had enough surprises in their lives.

(The men go off together while BETH sits down on the lawn chaise and MUFFIE stares at her.)

MUFFIE

You don't truly mean to marry him, do you?

BETH

Who knows? Certainly not me. But I do like him enormously. Just as I realized that I was so much less than I thought myself to be, I find a man who is so much more than I ever dreamed he could be. Generous, gentle, obedient –

MUFFIE

Sure. I can see what you like about him. After you scrape off the surface grit there's a lovely, shiny man inside, but it will never work out for you. It will be far worse when you clean him up. Once when I was feeling broke – I'd overdrawn on my trust as usual – I decided to sell those rare eighteenth century dining chairs and table that I kept in storage. The family jewels. All that elegant Philadelphia provenance, lion's claw foot and other bullshit carving. When I lifted the sheets it looked so disgustingly worn that I had the set refinished before I called in the dealer. He shook his head in sad disapproval and told me that I had diminished their value by tens of thousands by having them cleaned and restored. Your Jerry is like that. If you refinish him, he may gleam but he loses half his value for you.

(*A beat*)

You have something you want to tell me?

BETH

No.

MUFFIE

Fuck want to. Have to?

BETH

Yes.

MUFFIE

Then do so before it devours you. I'm the only one in the world you can tell because nobody would believe me if I spilled the beans. You really don't have to tell me. I know.

BETH

I figured you would.

MUFFIE

When did you find it?

BETH

The morning after.

MUFFIE

Where?

BETH

Under his pillow. He knew I always made the bed in our room. It was more a suicide memo than a note. Written on one of those note pads you get from Save the Wildlife people with a cuddly cartoon bear on it. Everyone throws them out – but not David. From the desk of David Grauer it read – beneath the adorable bear.

MUFFIE

Yes?

BETH

"Beth, apologies worthless, but so deeply sorry. You'll find a life insurance policy in the top draw of the breakfront in the breakfast room. I took it out years ago when the girls were born. You're the sole beneficiary. The premiums are all paid up. Five million will more than cover expenses and the girl's education. Please, don't blame yourself. I know what I did and I know what I am doing. Be good to the girls. And destroy this note. No nonsense. Love you, David."

MUFFIE

My poor baby. What did you do with it?

BETH

Burned it. Tore through the goddamned house looking for a pack of dry matches. The first old paper pack I found was damp, wouldn't strike, but finally I located an old box of wooden kitchen matches. And lo and behold they made a fire. You don't know how hard the world has become since everyone has stopped smoking. No fresh matches to be found easily. But I found them.

MUFFIE

Good. You did right. I might have torn it up and swallowed the tiny pieces, but burning is good too.

BETH

It was a crime. The insurance would never have paid out if there was proof of his suicide. And that was –

MUFFIE

It's what anyone would do.

BETH

I am not anyone. I am me. Elizabeth Hamilton. That bastard, David. Even in death he made me an accomplice to a crime. He punished me by bringing me down to where I've never been. I committed a crime, Muffie. A real crime. Fraud. I don't know who I am since David...

MUFFIE

...had his accident. That's what it was. That's what it is. That's what it will always be. The rest is a grieving widow's unhinged delusions.
(Wrapping her arms around BETH.)
Sweet girl of mine. Forget about that note. It's apple time. You may not think you know who you are but I know! So don't be a winesap.

BETH

(Trying to recover)

What shall I reach for? A fortune?

MUFFIE

Sweet and aromatic variety. Softer the longer it's left on the tree. Tastes like Benedictine liquor.

BETH

Remarkably resistant to disease, except for European canker, for which it is irritatingly susceptible.

MUFFIE

Whose fortune? Jerry's?

BETH

I don't think so. Although he's very nice. Too nice for people like us.

MUFFIE

You could break his heart? That could keep you busy and out of trouble. He clearly adores you. And his looks have definitely improved as owner of this house. You could train him like a rescue dog and he'd be ever so grateful.

BETH

No point in going down that path again. Maybe I'll take the girls to Europe.

MUFFIE

Oh? I like that.

BETH

The old travel cure. It worked for me after my divorce. Leon's image kept hanging around so stubbornly when I was in France, he hung there in the grey Paris sky like a palimpsest. But I could barely remember him by the time I got to Prague and by the time I reached Vienna I had forgotten him completely with the first taste of the Sacher-Tortes. I lost all memory of that pretentious shit. But I gained five pounds.

MUFFIE

Speaking of Europe and of shits, do you know who's been calling me day and night? You'll never guess. Yes you will, so I better tell you first. That Polish bastard, Kaminsky. Probably broke again. I was so lonely I was going to answer his call today. But I won't. Not now. Who needs husbands or lovers when you have a friend? I know! We can go to Berlin together. I was there last year and I loved it. Handsome blonde doormen smiling their best socialized dentistry at you, and little old Turkish beggar women huddled in doorways like a bag or black rags waiting to be photographed. You can even bring a dog into a restaurant.

BETH

I don't have a dog.

MUFFIE

I'll buy one in Berlin. It'll give the girls a companion when we're off trolling for men and museums. A dog that needs love and bratwurst. We'll do Europe as it's supposed to be done. The girls will adore the Zoo, and we'll set them loose in the KaDeWe with a credit card and they'll eat and buy and eat and buy and you and I will have all those concerts and galleries. You must go! It's arranged. You owe it to yourself to take a holiday. Fuck holiday. Run away. Darling, if anyone has the right, you've earned it. Fraud is such hard work when you have no practice and a foolish conscience.

BETH

You think I can do this?

MUFFIE

We can do anything. Look, I have the car keys. I can drive us back to the city now, leaving Einhorn and Jerry here. And tomorrow we can escape to Europe.

BETH

I couldn't.

MUFFIE

Yes, you can. We can be strolling Unter den Linden by tomorrow evening. We could be young again. Or pretend that we are before we grow old. Our senior year abroad. Bethie, it will save your life.

(BETH looks at MUFFIE, takes her arm, and they exit together breaking into a run.)

LIGHTS OUT

Sherman Yellen, playwright, librettist, screen-writer, lyricist and now memoirist, was nominated for a Tony Award for his book for the 1970 musical *The Rothschilds*, with a score by *Fiddler on the Roof* songwriters Jerry Bock and Sheldon Harnick. Sherman wrote the libretto for the Will Holt and Gary William Freidman musical *Treasure Island*, winner of the Broadway World Best Regional musical Award (2012). Among his many theater works is his satirical sketch "Delicious Indignities" which appeared in the New York and London revue *Oh! Calcutta!* His straight plays on and off Broadway include *New Gods for Lovers, Strangers,* and *December Fools*.

Sherman was librettist and lyricist for *Josephine Tonight*, an original musical he wrote with the late composer Wally Harper about the early life of Josephine Baker, which *The Chicago Sun-Times* called "a shining new musical" and which the DC press praised for being "so hot that it sizzles."

In his youth he worked as a librettist with legendary composer Richard Rodgers. Together with Sheldon Harnick they recently revised the Rodgers-Harnick musical *Rex* about Henry VIII. This new version had a successful premiere in Toronto.

His teleplays have won him two Emmy Awards and a Peabody Award, first for his *John Adams, Lawyer* in the PBS series *The Adams Chronicles*, and later for *An Early Frost*, a groundbreaking drama about AIDS in America broadcast on NBC, as well as an Emmy Nomination for his *Hallmark Hall of Fame* version of *Beauty and the Beast* starring George C. Scott. Sherman's screenplay adaptations of classic novels range from *Great Expectations* to *Phantom of the Opera*. He has received awards in Arts and Letters from Bard College, and he is a frequent contributor of essays on the arts, literature, and politics to online publications such as *The Huffington Post*.

Sherman recently published his autobiographical novella *Cousin Bella – The Whore of Minsk*, available in a volume which also includes his holiday short story *A Christmas Lilly*. He is currently completing his memoir *Spotless*, a recreation of his New York childhood in the 1930s and '40s and his young adulthood in the 1950s, which will be published later this year.

Sherman is married, the father of two sons, Nicholas and Christopher, and has three much loved granddaughters. He has lived in London and Los Angeles, worked in Berlin and Budapest, but home was, is, and always will be New York City.

Also Recommended

Cousin Bella – The Whore of Minsk recounts the life of a young Jewish woman in Tsarist Russia who was sold into prostitution, rescued by the author's indomitable grandmother, and then immigrated to America where the most extraordinary drama of her life was yet to unfold. Written by Tony® nominee and two-time Emmy® winning screenwriter, Sherman Yellen. Also included is Yellen's holiday classic, *A Christmas Lilly*, a tender, poignant memory of a Jewish family's first Christmas tree in 1939, celebrating the author's wise and compassionate mother.

Trade Paperback ISBN-13: 978-1495290435 Paperback $8.95
Also Available in **Kindle eBook** and **Unabridged Audiobook**

MORECLACKE PUBLISHING

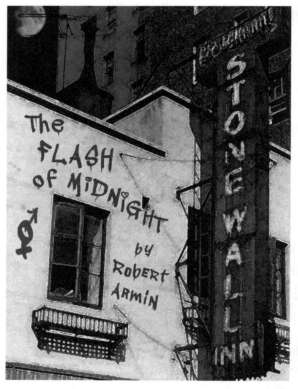

Also Recommended

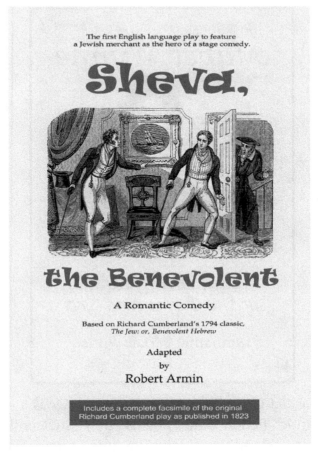

Sheva, the Benevolent is a faithful adaptation of Richard Cumberland's 1794 comedy, *The Jew: or, Benevolent Hebrew,* featuring Sheva, the first Jewish moneylender to be portrayed as the hero of a stage comedy. Includes a Preface by playwright Robert Armin, an introduction by 18th Century theater scholar Jean Marsden, and a high quality facsimile of the original play as published in 1823.

Trade Paperback ISBN-13: 978-0615663166 Paperback $11.95
Also Available in **Kindle eBook** (without facsimile)

MORECLACKE **PUBLISHING**

Also Recommended

Mabel Wynne

and Other Tales
of the Romantic Era

by

Nathaniel Parker Willis

Edited and Introduced by Robert Armin

Mabel Wynne and Other Tales of the Romantic Age is a selection of short romantic fiction and poems by Nineteenth Century American writer, editor, journalist and international travel correspondent, Nathaniel Parker Willis (1806-1867), newly edited and introduced by novelist Robert Armin. Beautifully illustrated with rare etchings and decorative drop cap lettering all reproduced from vintage books of the period. Also included are five essays by Willis on the American Woman, as originally published in the *New York Mirror* and *The Home Journal*.

Trade Paperback ISBN-13: 978-1499187229 Paperback $9.95
Also Available in Kindle eBook and Audiobook

MORECLACKE PUBLISHING

COMING IN FEBRUARY 2015

The Used and Abused is a fresh retelling of Fyodor Dostoyevsky's early novel, *The Insulted and Injured*, which drew heavily upon the writings of Charles Dickens for its inspiration. A frustrated love affair, an orphan girl in distress, a scheming aristocrat, and an angry father who casts his daughter out of his life, are just a few of the ingredients that make this little known Russian novel a delight to read. More than simply a new translation, novelist Robert Armin has expanded upon and enhanced the characters and dialogue of Dostoyevsky' original Russian novel to give modern readers a full and engaging reading experience from beginning to end.

Trade Paperback ISBN-13: 978-0996016919 Paperback $17.95
Also Available in Kindle eBook and Audiobook

MORECLACKE PUBLISHING

CPSIA information can be obtained
at www.ICGtesting.com
Printed in the USA
FSHW021502221219
65367FS